With The 4th Battalion The Cameronians, Scottish Rifles, In South Africa, 1900-1901

Arthur Henry Courtenay

With

The 4th Battalion The Cameronians (Scottish Rifles) in South Africa, *1900–1901.*

BY

COLONEL ARTHUR HENRY COURTENAY, C.B.,

COMMANDANT.

PRINTED FOR THE AUTHOR BY

WILLIAM BROWN,

26 PRINCES STREET, EDINBURGH.

1905.

PREFACE.

THIS book is published with the object of placing on permanent record the services, at a time of national emergency, of the 4th Battalion The Cameronians (Scottish Rifles).

It is merely a chronicle, with no claim to style and literary merit, and avoiding all criticism of the operations.

Though intended primarily for the Officers, Non-commissioned Officers, and Men of the Battalion, and their friends, should others beyond that limited sphere find interest in its pages, it will be very gratifying to the compiler, who here desires to gratefully acknowledge the assistance he has received in the preparation of its pages from Lieut.-Colonel R. M. HOLDEN, his present Second in Command, and from Captain A. F. TOWNSHEND, who was his Staff Officer at Boshof for close upon a year.

1st July, 1905.

CONTENTS.

WITH THE

4TH BATTALION THE CAMERONIANS

(SCOTTISH RIFLES)

IN SOUTH AFRICA, 1900-1901.

————◆————

CHAPTER I.

(12th December 1899 to 15th August 1900.)

EMBODIMENT—ORDERED TO SOUTH AFRICA—OPERATIONS IN THE ORANGE FREE STATE.

TO describe the many differences which resulted in war between the British and the Dutch for supremacy in South Africa would be too long a story to relate here; and it will suffice to say that the determination of the Boers to fight, if necessary, for their independence dates probably from 1881, when, after our arms had suffered defeat at Laing's Nek and Majuba, a peace, detrimental to the British reputation and discreditable to the Government of the day, was concluded, which, it is not too much to say, has ever since rankled in the breast of the British soldier. Matters were not improved by the badly-planned and unsuccessful raid, headed by Dr. Jameson, in 1895; but the climax was

B

reached when, with the obvious intention of provoking hostilities, the Boers issued an ultimatum to Great Britain in 1899, the period for compliance with which expired on the 11th of October. Great Britain entered upon the war which ensued unprepared, and in ignorance of the power of her enemy, with the result that the largest and the best equipped armies which have ever left her shores were brought to a standstill, foiled and humiliated, with the loss of many thousands of prisoners, killed, and wounded. And this by a nation of peasants who had never worn a uniform in their lives, who were ignorant of strategy and tactics, and who apparently had nothing in their favour but their mobility, a knowledge of the country in which they were fighting, and a familiarity with the use of the rifle. On the receipt at home of the news of the first disasters, Lord Roberts was appointed Commander-in-Chief in South Africa, with Lord Kitchener as his Chief of the Staff, and reinforcements were hurriedly despatched to the country. This was the state of affairs when the British Government found it necessary to call upon the Militia, the oldest military body in the kingdom, a force which has never failed to render good service in time of national emergency—a fact soon forgotten—to fulfil the purposes of its existence as the support of the Regular army. The 4th Battalion of the Cameronians, or to use its more familiar title, Scottish Rifles, was embodied for permanent duty for the third time in the course of its existence, and assembled at its headquarters at Hamilton, in Lanarkshire, on the 12th of December, 1899, under the command of Colonel A. H. Courtenay, commandant of the 3rd and 4th battalions of the regiment. Colonel Courtenay was no stranger to his command; he had served in the regiment for nearly twenty-nine years, had been Lieut.-Colonel of a battalion from 1891 to 1895, since which the two Militia battalions had been under his command.

The 4th Battalion proceeded on the day of its embodiment to Maryhill Barracks, Glasgow, and very shortly afterwards volunteered for service anywhere abroad, though the men's conditions of enlistment rendered them liable for home service only. In January, 1900, the commanding officer was asked by the War Office authorities, by wire, to ascertain if the battalion·would volunteer for service in South Africa, which the officers, N.C.O.'s, and men at once consented to do, and were forthwith placed under orders to proceed to the seat of war.

The battalion left Glasgow on the 19th February, 1900, for Southampton, and embarked there on the following morning in the transport *Cephalonia*. The officers accompanying the battalion to South Africa were Colonel A. H. Courtenay, commanding; Major and Hon. Lieut.-Col. Montague Johnstone (late Major, Royal Scots Greys), and Major H. Chavasse; Captains H. M. Clifford, A. R. Littledale, D. Blaikie-Hislop, C. J. Lynch, V. A. Blake, D. C. Burns-Macdonald, H. H. Protheroe Smith, and A. F. Townsend (late Lieutenant, 2nd Battalion); Lieutenants and Second-Lieutenants, M. H. D. Thomson-Carmichael, R. Brudenell Murphy, G. Hazlerigg, G. F. Phillips, A. F. Lumsden, R. Glossop, R. F. Forbes, H. Boyd-Rochfort, F. H. Bridgman, D. H. Thorburn, J. D. Anderson, B. C. M. Maxwell-Heron, and A. H. Seagrim; and Captain and Adjutant C. M. S. Henning; while Captain T. K. Gardner, 2nd Volunteer Battalion the

Highland Light Infantry, and Lieutenant S. M. Castle, 6th Battalion the Royal Fusiliers, were attached for duty and accompanied the battalion to South Africa. Civil-Surgeon T. Inverarity was also attached, and Captain Blaikie-Hislop acted as Quartermaster, pending the arrival at Kimberley of Lieutenant and Quartermaster W. Taylor. The total strength on embarkation amounted to 28 officers, and 543 warrant officers, non-commissioned officers, and men.

The following troops also embarked on the *Cephalonia*, the whole being under the command of Colonel A. H. Courtenay, viz. :—The 3rd Battalion "The Queen's" (Royal West Surrey Regiment), under command of Colonel F. H. Fairtlough ; details of the 2nd Battalion Scottish Rifles, under Captain M. L. Pears ; details of the 2nd Battalion "The Queen's," under Captain R. Alexander, 1st Battalion Rifle Brigade ; one Telegraph Section, Royal Engineers ; two typists for Lord Roberts' Staff; and No. 8 General Hospital, under Lieut.-Col. Beamish and Major Edeye of the Royal Army Medical Corps.

After calling at St. Vincent to coal, the *Cephalonia* arrived in Table Bay on the 21st March, but did not go into the docks until the 24th.

The troops were disembarked on the 26th March, and the 4th Battalion Scottish Rifles was at once entrained for Kimberley, which had been relieved by Major-General French on the 15th of February. It arrived there on the 29th and was sent on to Dronfield, seven miles north of the town, and was posted to the 1st Division (Lieut.-General Lord Methuen, K.C.V.O., C.B., C.M.G.), and formed part of the 9th Brigade, commanded by Major-General C. W. H. Douglas, late Gordon Highlanders.

The battalion was inspected at Dronfield by Lord Methuen on the 31st March, and proceeded by march-route, with the 9th Brigade, to Boshof, in the Orange Free State, on the 2nd of April, arriving there on the 4th, and pitching camp with the remainder of the 1st Division close to the town.

The engagement with Villebois-de-Marueil's commando took place at Driefontein, near Boshof, on the 5th of April, when Villebois was killed, and his whole force taken prisoners. In his pocket was found a plan of attack * for the retaking of the town of Boshof, which was handed to Colonel Courtenay, with orders to prepare the defences accordingly. General Villebois-de-Marueil † was buried in the cemetery at Boshof on the 6th April, together with Lieutenants C. Boyle and Williams, Sergeant Patrick Campbell, of the Imperial Yeomanry, and others killed in action on the same occasion.

On the arrival of the battalion at Boshof, orders were received from Lord Methuen to detail two officers and sixty men to escort an ox convoy to Kimberley, a distance of thirty-five miles, and return at once with supplies. Captain C. J. Lynch and Lieutenant R. Glossop were detailed for this duty, and brought their convoy back in safety. They remained on convoy duty until the return of the battalion from Kimberley to Boshof in May, and had to undergo much hardship and long and tiring marches, &c.

On the 1st Division proceeding to Swartzkoppiefontein,

* For a copy of the plan, see Appendix No. A.

† General Villebois-de-Marueil was a French officer serving with the Boer forces. A memorial stone was subsequently placed over his grave by Lord Methuen.

about twelve miles north of Boshof, on the 7th April, Colonel Courtenay was left in command at Boshof with his own battalion, the 3rd Battalion South Wales Borderers, under Lieut.-Col. C. Healy, and other troops. He received the following orders in writing from Lord Methuen on taking over the command :—

1.

"The Officer Commanding at Boshof will without delay arrange with the Engineer Officer left at Boshof a scheme of defence of the town, which can only be taken by an attack at night. In order that he may look at this question from the point of view of the enemy, he is to read the plan of attack made out by General Villebois, and make up his mind how best to meet it. There will be at first two battalions at Boshof, and 150 mounted troops, one battery of Field Artillery, and a section of Howitzers; but later on this force will be increased.

"The garrison should thoroughly understand its duties on the 'Alarm' sounding. If the outpost line is intelligently posted, and its duties properly carried out, the town should not be exposed to danger.

"(Sgd.) METHUEN, Lieut.-Gen.,
"*Commanding 1st Division.*

"BOSHOF, *6th April,* 1900."

2.

"*To Officer Commanding, Boshof.*

"You will have sufficient mounted troops in Boshof to reconnoitre some distance from the town, not only to protect the line of communications, particularly towards the east and south, but also to gather in from the farm-houses forage and food. Many of these houses are well stored, and it is essential that I should economise the forage and food stored here. The grazing is bad, and the mounted troops will have to go out some distance to graze their horses.

" You are to keep me informed as regularly as you can of the condition of affairs here. If you find any person in any way inciting the enemy, or if you have any suspicion of his being a person likely to incite people against us, your duty is at once to send him on parole to Cape Town, or send him as a prisoner.

"(Sgd.) METHUEN, Lieut.-Gen.,
"*Commanding 1st Division.*

" BOSHOF, *7th April,* 1900."

" I enclose a copy of a telegram from the Commander-in-Chief received last night. Please endeavour to carry out the instructions without delay.

"(Sgd.) M."

On the 9th April the C.O. received orders to send two companies to Frankfort, an important post commanding the road between Kimberley and Boshof, and a pass about two and a-half miles long between very high and steep kopjes. Captain T. K. Gardner, Lieutenant Castle, and Second Lieutenants Lumsden and Anderson were detailed for this duty with F and H Companies. Captain Gardner received his orders from the Chief Staff Officer, 1st Division, which were to hold the pass to enable convoys to get from Kimberley to Boshof. Arriving at Frankfort on the 10th April, he and his detachment proceeded to fortify the kopje he selected as most suitable, and remained there until relieved on the 17th April by a detachment of the 3rd Battalion South Wales Borderers under Major Morgan. On the 19th April he rejoined headquarters at Kimberley (escorting an empty convoy there from Frankfort), the battalion having proceeded there.

On the 10th April, Colonel Courtenay received orders from Lord Methuen to march to Kimberley with his battalion that afternoon, the inhabitants of that place being under the impression that the Boers contemplated renewing hostilities in the neighbourhood. Having bivouacked that night at Leeuwfontein, and outspanned at Slabbert's Farm the following day, the battalion arrived at Tolpan in a very heavy thunder-storm at about 9 P.M. on the 11th, thus performing a very creditable march of thirty miles in about twenty-four hours. On the following morning, the 12th, they marched into Kimberley, five miles off, and encamped at Newton Camp. On the same day the battalion received orders to garrison five redoubts round Kimberley—viz., Kenilworth, Premier Mine, and Nos. 1, 2, and 3 Redoubts.

About 1st May a detachment of the battalion was ordered to escort a convoy of stores from Kimberley to Frankfort. The convoy comprised seven steam traction engines, and the escort consisted of eighty-two men of the battalion under Captains Blaikie-Hislop, Mellish,* and Burns-Macdonald, and Lieutenants Castle, Lumsden, and Seagrim; 30 Yeomanry, under Lieut.-Colonel Meyrick,† were to meet the convoy half-way, and scout the country from there to Frankfort.

The roads were sandy and heavy, and the engines constantly broke down. At sun-down the engines were laagered up, with the exception of one left about a mile behind, stuck fast in the sand, an officer and ten men being left in charge of it, and bringing it on at daybreak. A patrol of the enemy came

---

* Captain R. W. Mellish had recently joined the battalion at Kimberley, from England.

† Lieut.-Colonel F. C. Meyrick, Pembrokeshire Yeomanry, late Major 15th Hussars, and previously a lieutenant in the 4th Scottish Rifles in 1881–84.

down quite close to it at midnight, but beat a hasty retreat on seeing one of the trucks occupied. Next day the whole convoy was taken safely in to Frankfort, the infantry escort handing it over to the Yeomanry at Koodoosdam, at the entrance to Frankfort Pass. Owing to a misunderstanding the ration wagon of the 4th Scottish Rifles went on ahead too far, and failed to return, and except for a few biscuits given them by an hospital convoy returning from Boshof with sick and wounded, the men had nothing to eat for thirty-six hours. Captain Blaikie-Hislop gave them the option of waiting on the chance of the return of the wagon, or of marching back to Kimberley at once. They chose the latter alternative, and performed the sixteen miles, with two short halts, arriving at Newton Camp in excellent condition. During its stay at Kimberley the battalion was transferred from the 9th to the 20th Brigade, under Major-General A. H. Paget, late Scots Guards. Nothing of any importance occurred at Kimberley while the battalion was there, beyond several false alarms, including one on the night of the 22nd April, when the enemy were reported in force at Frankfort, and the battalion was in readiness to proceed there on the following morning. While at Kimberley Lieutenant W. M. Russell joined the battalion in charge of its machine gun (Vickers-Maxim) and party, which he had brought out from England.

On the 8th May, at twelve midnight, the battalion received orders to prepare to march to Boshof to join the 20th Brigade. In the meantime the 1st Division under Lord Methuen were occupied with the enemy in the neighbourhood of Swartzkoppiefontein, and subsequently returned to Boshof. On the 9th May the Adjutant, Sergeant-Major, and Orderly Room Clerk were all in hospital, the Quarter-master Lieutenant W. Taylor, 1st Battalion Scottish Rifles, who had recently been appointed, arrived from home. Captain A. F. Townsend performed the duties of Adjutant while the 4th Battalion Scottish Rifles were at Kimberley.

On the morning of the 10th May, at 4 A.M., the battalion marched out of Newton Camp, Kimberley, brigaded with the 4th Battalion South Staffordshire Regiment, under Colonel F. Charington, the whole being under the command of Colonel A. H. Courtenay. The battalion outspanned at Hulls Farm, and were joined there by a troop of Imperial Yeomanry, bivouacked at Frankfort at 9 P.M., and on the following morning proceeded to Slabbert's Farm; in the evening they marched to Leeuwfontein, where the troops bivouacked, and marched into Boshof on the following morning (12th May), and joined the 1st Division, 20th Brigade, which latter consisted of—4 Squadrons Imperial Yeomanry; 38th Battery R.F.A.; 2nd Battalion King's Own Yorkshire Light Infantry; 1st Battalion Royal Munster Fusiliers; 4th Battalion Scottish Rifles; 4th Battalion South Staffordshire Regiment, and Departmental Corps.

On the arrival of the battalion at Frankfort on the 10th May, *en route* to Boshof, Captain Clifford was detailed as Officer-Commanding at Frankfort until all troops had passed through to join Lord Methuen's Column at Boshof. Captain Clifford had with him two companies of the battalion, under Captain Protheroe Smith and Lieutenants R. Brudenell Murphy and G. Hazlerigg; one section of the Diamond Fields Artillery, under Lieutenant Faulkener; one troop Yeomanry, under Lieutenant Crabbe; one troop, under Lieutenant Sir E. H. Hulse, Bart.; and a third troop, under

Lieutenant Viner Johnson. Captain Clifford's orders were to occupy the pass and hold it with his infantry whenever a convoy was reported to be arriving, which occurred almost daily. The two companies of the battalion under his command (B and C) had a very trying time in consequence, relieving each other morning and night, the Yeomanry being engaged scouting. On the 13th May, Captain Clifford received orders to march to Boshof with all the troops at Frankfort. He arrived at Boshof on the morning of the 15th. Captain Protheroe Smith was left behind, suffering from dysentery.

On the 13th May the battalion received orders from Lieut.-General Lord Methuen that, on the departure from Boshof of the 1st Division, four companies of the battalion should accompany the 20th Brigade, the remainder of the battalion to form portion of the garrison of Boshof, of which Colonel A. H. Courtenay was appointed Commandant.

Captain T. K. Gardner and Lieutenant S. M. Castle* were attached to the 1st Battalion Northumberland Fusiliers, with the 9th Brigade.

On the 14th May, Captain Henning, adjutant of the battalion, rejoined from sick leave, and on the same day the 9th Brigade marched out of Boshof under command of Major-General Douglas, Lord Methuen accompanying it; and on the following day the 20th Brigade, commanded by Major-General A. H. Paget, late Scots Guards, marched out of Boshof.

Captain C. J. Lynch and 2nd Lieutenant Boyd-Rochfort

---

* Lieutenant Castle was subsequently appointed to a Commission in the 2nd Battalion Royal Sussex Regiment.

were attached to the 1st Battalion Royal Munster Fusiliers with the 20th Brigade.

Since the arrival of Lord Roberts in the country, the prospects of the British army had brightened considerably. In addition to the relief of Kimberley, the fourth attempt to relieve Ladysmith had proved successful. Cronje had surrendered with his army at Paardeberg on the anniversary of Majuba, and on the 13th of March Lord Roberts entered Bloemfontein, the Boers retreating before his advance. Mafeking was relieved on 17th May, and on the 5th June Pretoria was occupied by the British forces. But there was very much yet to be accomplished all over the country. On the departure of the 1st Division from Boshof on the 14th and 15th May, 1900, Colonel Courtenay having been appointed Commandant, with Captain J. Campbell Gardner and Captain D. Blaikie-Hislop as his Staff and Intelligence Officers respectively, Major Chavasse assumed command of the six companies of the 4th Scottish Rifles in the town.

The following orders were given to Colonel A. H. Courtenay on the departure of the Division :—

" *Pressing.*
" *O.C. Boshof (Colonel Courtenay, 4th Scottish Rifles).*

" 1. The garrison of Boshof, during the absence of the column, will consist of—5 companies South Wales Borderers ; 6 companies Scottish Rifles ; 3 troops Imperial Yeomanry ; 1 section 38th Battery R.F.A., and details of units of the Division.

" 2. The outlying posts marked in attached map will be given up, and only Kopjes Nos. IX. and IV. will be occupied, each by one Company, night and day.

" Examining Guards are to be stationed at the main entrance ·on each of the four sides of the town, the remaining entrances being blocked. No persons are permitted to enter or leave without passes. All civilian wagons and vehicles entering to be searched for spirits, and all outgoing vehicles for food stuffs. No spirits are allowed to be brought into the town, and only one bag of meal is allowed to be taken out by each farmer every ten days, other food stuffs in proportion.

"3. Other outposts round the town by night, and Cossack posts by day, on distant kopjes, can be furnished at your discretion.

"4. You will nominate an Officer to act as Staff-Officer.

"5. Certain shelter trenches have been prepared with a view to defence of town. In case of attack, the line to be held must be decided on by you. Where there are no shelter trenches, the outer walls of the town are suitable for defence.

"6. You will pay special attention to the sanitation of the camps, and to guard against pollution of water supply.

"7. A large scale map, showing the range to conspicuous points, is forwarded herewith.

"8. Half the tents of units proceeding with the division are to be left standing. These you will cause to be struck and stored, with any surplus baggage, being careful that they are not destroyed by white ants.

"9. A scheme for the defence of Boshof is forwarded herewith.

"10. You are to nominate an officer for Intelligence purposes.

"By Order,

"(Signed) H. E. BELFIELD, Colonel A.A.G.,
" *Chief Staff-Officer.*

"BOSHOF, 13*th May*, 1900."

As a matter of fact, the troops left under Colonel A. H. Courtenay's command were as follows :—2 officers and 62 N.C.O.'s and men, 38th Battery R.F.A., with 2 guns; 1 officer and 28 N.C.O.'s and men, Diamond Fields Artillery, with 2 guns; 1 officer and 49 N.C.O.'s and men, 58th Company Imperial Yeomanry; 13 officers and 228 N.C.O.'s and men, 3rd Battalion South Wales Borderers; 21 officers and

284 N.C.O.'s and men, 4th Battalion Scottish Rifles; 6 officers and 658 N.C.O.'s and men, details of units of the 1st Division (including 1st Battalion Northumberland Fusiliers, 1st Battalion Loyal North Lancashire Regiment, 2nd Battalion Northamptonshire Regiment, 2nd Battalion King's Own Yorkshire Light Infantry; 1st Battalion Royal Munster Fusiliers; and 4th Battalion South Staffordshire Regiment); 3 officers and 55 N.C.O.'s and men of the Royal Engineers, Army Service Corps, and Royal Army Medical Corps. Total—48 officers and 1370 N.C.O.'s and men.

The first orders issued by the Commandant were as follows, and will show the dispositions, &c., made :—

"Boshof, 16th May, 1900.

"*Station Orders by Colonel A. H. Courtenay, Commandant, Boshof.*

"1. Countersign, 'Glasgow.'

"2. The details of the Yorkshire Light Infantry, and 2nd Lieutenant Wise and details of the Munster Fusiliers, will be attached to the 4th Battalion Scottish Rifles, from this date; details of all other infantry battalions will be attached to the South Wales Borderers.

"All Yeomanry details will be attached to the 58th Company Imperial Yeomanry, under command of Lieutenant Viner Johnson.

"3. The south side of the town of Boshof, including the magazine and west kopjes, will be held by the South Wales Borderers and details attached; the north side of the town and the green kopje will be held by the Scottish Rifles and details attached.

"The boundary between the two positions will be the road running through the centre of the town, east and west, which will be held by the Scottish Rifles. Commanding Officers will make arrangements as to entrenchments, outposts, picquets, and sentries for their own units, reporting to the Commandant with reference thereto. In the event of an attack on the town, the entrenchments will be the first line of defence, and the walls of the town the second. Officers commanding will have picquet parades for the purpose of stationing the men under their command at such points of the lines of defence (first and second) as will be occupied by them in the event of an attack.

"Should an attack be threatened, the bugles will sound 'the alarm' at whichever side the town is threatened. And 'the alarm' will be repeated at the opposite side. The bell on the market square will be rung sharply. All troops will immediately stand to arms, and proceed to the stations occupied by them in practice.

"Piquets and sentries will hold their ground as long as possible before falling back on the main body.

"Sentries will at all times be alert and vigilant, carefully observing any noise denoting the presence of the enemy.

"This is particularly necessary at night, and should any unusual noise, such as sounds of men or horses approaching, be heard, sentries should at once alarm the picquets quietly, and they should, if necessary, alarm the guard or main body.

"Sentries must halt all parties when some distance from their posts, and any person unable to give the countersign should be handed over to the guard.

"Examining posts will be stationed at the main entrance on each of the four sides of the town, the remaining entrances being blocked. The examining post on the south side will be furnished by the South Wales Borderers, those on the other three sides by the 4th Scottish Rifles. It will be the strict duty of these examining posts to permit no person, on any account, to enter or leave the town at any hour without a pass ; to search all wagons and vehicles of every sort, the property of civilians entering the town, for spirits ; and all outgoing wagons and vehicles for food.

"Should vehicles containing spirits be found coming in, or vehicles containing food be found going out, they are to be sent at once to the Commandant, Civil Administrator (Captain Ross), or Intelligence Officer (Captain Blaikie-Hislop), who will deal with them.

" 4. Officers in charge of the magazine, west and green kopjes will be most particular, and keep a good look-out during the day with field glasses, for any sign of the enemy, and are to report at once (should they see any) to the Commandant, and to their own companies. All officers will be most particular, day and night, to see that sentries are thoroughly acquainted with their duties and orders.

"5. The O.C. Imperial Yeomanry will make arrangements for Cossack posts on the distant kopjes indicated to him, and will also make arrangements as to his men sending immediate information to the Commandant, should they observe any signs of the enemy.

"6. In the event of a threatened attack, and the 'alarm' sounding, the Commandant and staff will proceed to the Church Square, and will be found there, if required, to give orders pending the development of the attack.

"7. Orders as to sanitation, water supply, &c.

"8. No women or children will be permitted to leave Boshof without a special pass, signed by the District Commissioner (Captain Ross).

"9. The Commandant appeals with confidence to all ranks, to exercise that vigilance and care so essential in an enemy's country, and to treat the inhabitants of Boshof with every courtesy and consideration in their power.

· "10. Officers commanding will send a N.C.O. daily to the Headquarter Office Landdrost, at 5 P.M., to receive station orders.

"By Order,

"(Sgd.) J. C. GARDNER,* *Captain,*
" *Station Staff Officer.*"

It was known that after the departure of the Division

---

* Captain James Campbell Gardner, who had up to this time served in South Africa with the first Canadian Contingent, belonged to the 3rd Battalion Scottish Rifles. He joined the 4th Battalion at Kimberley in May, from which date he was attached for duty to that battalion.

from Boshof, an attack on that place was contemplated by the Boers, and the troops at once proceeded to make the necessary defences. The following reports from the Commandant to the G.O.C. 1st Division, dated 3rd and 26th June respectively, show the state of affairs, and what occurred at Boshof up to the latter date, including the surrender of over 600 of the enemy.

" From Colonel A. H. COURTENAY,
 " *4th Battalion The Cameronians (Scottish Rifles),*
  " *Commandant, Boshof.*
"To the C.S.O., FIRST DIVISION,
 " S.A.F.F., Kroonstad.

      " BOSHOF, *3rd June,* 1900.

" SIR,—I have the honour to report for the information of the G.O.C. 1st Division, as follows :—

" 1. In pursuance of the orders you left with me, dated 13th May.

"I took over the command of this garrison on the 14th May, and arranged, in accordance therewith, a scheme for defence of the town, based on the plan forwarded to me by the G.O.C.

"I nominated Captain J. C. Gardner and Captain Blaikie-Hislop, 4th Battalion Scottish Rifles, to act as staff-officer and officer for Intelligence purposes respectively.

" I issued orders with reference to the defence of the town in case of attack, and the sanitation of the camps, &c., and I caused all the tents left standing by the Division, which were not required, to be struck.

" 2. For several days after the departure of the Division there were persistent rumours of a contemplated attack upon the town, and on the 18th May, the officer in charge of the magazine kopje and others reported seeing large bodies of men advancing north and east of the town, six or seven miles out.

" On the alarm sounding, all the troops were at their appointed stations : tents were struck, and everything was in readiness for an attack, within ten minutes.

"I rode out about three miles with Captain Ross, District Commissioner, but could see no trace of the enemy.

"From information I received from some of the Boers who afterwards surrendered, I believe they retired behind a kopje some distance out, to consult as to what course they would adopt.

"3. On the 19th May, a large number of Boers came in and surrendered with their arms, ammunition, and horses, and I passed them on to the District Commissioner, who administered to them the oath of allegiance, and gave them instructions as to their future conduct, and passes to return to their farms.

"This he has done in the case of all who have since surrendered.

"4. Among those who surrendered were the Commandant Du Plessis, and Field-Cornets H. Du Plessis, Fraser, and Botha, who afforded the District Commissioner and myself a good deal of useful information, and I allowed them to remain on parole.

"The Military Governor, Bloemfontein, wired that these officers should be sent as prisoners of war, under escort, to Kimberley, and accordingly I sent them there on the 24th May, under charge of Captain MacDonald, 4th Battalion Scottish Rifles with written particulars, and a request to the Commandant, Kimberley, that they should be treated with every consideration, in consequence of their good behaviour while here.

"On his return here, Captain Burns-MacDonald reported to me that they had been sent straight to jail at Kimberley, and I wired in cypher to the chief of the staff, Army Headquarters, for the information of the Commander-in-Chief, that I did not consider that this course was likely to improve matters here.

"The Commander-in-Chief was good enough to wire to me personally, that he had ordered their immediate release on parole, and that he approved my action.

"Since that date, the Boers have been coming in in large numbers, and surrendering their arms, &c. Up to this day 564 have surrendered and have given up their arms and ammunition, and upwards of 406 horses, 8 mules, 123 oxen, 25 other cattle, and 571 sheep; 4 wagons, 6000 lbs. of corn, 3400 lbs. of maize and other goods, the property of the late Free State Government, have also been surrendered, and more are coming in daily.

"I am sending out patrols as often as possible to inspect farms in the neighbourhood, and to encourage the farmers to settle down, which they seem to be doing satisfactorily, but there are many complaints about the looting and depredations committed by natives, with which I am doing all in my power to deal ; but, as yet, no police have been sent from Bloemfontein as promised, and there are only 42 Imperial Yeomanry here now available for mounted duties.

"I would respectfully urge the necessity there is for establishing, as quickly as possible, a proper system of police in the outlying districts, not alone for the protection of property, but also to show the inhabitants that the British Government has really been established.

"5. On the 29th ult. the Military Governor, Bloemfontein, wired that 'Mr. Walker of Quaggashoek, a farm about forty miles east of Boshof, complained that some Zarps, with the notorious Vanderport, were recently visiting his farm.'

"The Military Governor requested 'that steps might be taken for their capture.' On the same day it was reported that the force in question was seventy or eighty strong.

"Having consulted with the District Commissioner, I organised a force of fifty Mounted Infantry from the 4th Battalion Scottish Rifles, 3rd South Wales Borderers, and other details of the 9th and 20th Brigades left here, mounted them on some of the horses surrendered by the Boers, and sent them on the morning of the 31st ult. to Quaggashoek, with one officer, details, and two guns R.F.A., one officer and details Imperial Yeomanry under command of Captain Henning, Adjutant 4th Scottish Rifles, with a view of capturing the party.

"I forward copy of my instructions to Captain Henning for the information of the G.O.C., and I hope Captain Henning will be successful in his mission ; but if not, I am confident it will have a good effect in the district.

"I expect my party back here on the 7th inst.

"6. I have already forwarded to you by wire (31st May, 1904) P. Howe's report as to the cannon supposed to be buried at Paardeberg.

"On the return of Captain Henning's party here, I propose, if approved, to send down a small party to investigate the place, where Howe states holes have been made.

"7. Pursuant to orders received from you, I sent all the tents and baggage belonging to the 1st Division, left behind here (except what are in use by the details here, and a small quantity of baggage left behind belonging to the Imperial Yeomanry which I shall forward by first opportunity), to Kroonstad *via* Kimberley. The South Wales Borderers and Scottish Rifles being the only exceptions.

"8. I regret to report that the sickness here has been very severe, and although over 100 convalescents have been sent to Kimberley within the last week, 9 officers and 106 N.C.O.'s and men still remain in hospital, most, if not all, suffering from Enteric or Dysentery.

"I have to report with deep regret the death of two officers, Lieutenant E. Mann, R.A.M.C., and 2nd Lieutenant W. H. Amedroz, 3rd South Wales Borderers, since I took over command, on the 14th ult.

"9. I have taken every precaution as regards the water being kept pure, and sanitation generally, and troops are still engaged in cleaning up the site of the camp of the south west of the town, part of which was left in a disgraceful state.

"It was impossible to get Kaffir labour for the purpose.

"I am glad to say fresh cases of illness have been much fewer during the last few days.

"The non-commissioned officer left in charge of supplies here was removed a few days after the Division left, and since then Quartermaster Sergeant Masters, a master baker, has been in charge, and has done all in his power to carry out the duties satisfactorily, but, as stated to you in my wire of the 2nd inst. (No. 117), and for the reason therein mentioned, I am dissatisfied with the A.S.C. arrangements here, and beg to request that an A.S.C. Officer may be sent as soon as possible, if only for a few days, to arrange matters connected with this department.

"The District Commissioner informs me that there are many liabilities (which have been incurred by the military authorities before and since I took over command) to be settled.

"The work here has been and is still very heavy; but, while

quite willing to undertake it and any responsibility I am equal to, I confess I am unable to cope with the A.S.C. arrangements.

"It appears to me most objectionable that the hospital authorities should have to get supplies of milk, eggs, &c., and give 'Chits' for them, instead of a proper and regular supply of such necessaries being provided for the sick, by contract or otherwise.

"I enclose letter from the P.M.O. on this subject.

"10. Trooper William Williams, Cape Police, Kimberley, arrived here from Hoopstad on the 30th ult., having been sent on here from that station, in a Cape cart, by Major Jones, Commanding 3rd South Wales Borderers. He made the statement, which I annex, and I considered it advisable to send him on at once to Kimberley, as he appeared to have other information which might be valuable.

"There was no convoy proceeding or likely to proceed to Kimberley for many days, and I therefore sent him by Cape cart, at a cost of £3, which the paymaster has refused to pay.

"I beg to request that the G.O.C. will be so good as to give directions for payment of the amount.

"11. I desire to express my highest appreciation of the manner in which Captain Ross, District Commissioner, has been good enough to advise and assist me in all matters of military administration since I took over command, and also to draw attention to the excellent work done by Captain Blaikie-Hislop, 4th Scottish Rifles, who has had most onerous and tedious work thrown upon him as Intelligence Officer, and in taking in arms, &c., and by Lieutenant Russell, 4th Scottish Rifles, who at the request of the District Commissioner has supervised the surrender of horses, cattle, &c., and has given entire satisfaction.

"I also wish to bear testimony to the valuable services rendered by Mr. Beck, his son, and Mr. P. Howe, who—especially the two first named—have acted as interpreters, for the District Commissioner and myself, all day long for many days, and have done all in their power to assist us.

"In conclusion, I have the greatest satisfaction in testifying to the excellent behaviour to the mixed body of troops (numbering over 1300 men drawn from different units) under my command ;

and expressing my thanks to the officers, N.C.O.'s, and men, for the manner in which they have carried out my orders.

 "I have the honour to be,
  "Sir,
   "Your obedient servant,
    "(Sgd.) ARTHUR H. COURTENAY,
   "Commanding 3rd and 4th Battalions Scottish Rifles.
    "Commandant, Boshof."

 "From Colonel A. H. COURTENAY, *Commandant, Boshof,*
 "To the C.S.O. FIRST DIVISION,
    "BOSHOF, 26*th June*, 1900.

 "SIR,—I have the honour to report for the information of the G.O.C. 1st Division, as follows :—

 "1. Since my last report, dated 3rd June, the inhabitants of this neighbourhood have continued to settle down, and most of them are now working on their farms.

 "Six hundred and five Burghers have surrendered here up to the present, and have given up their arms and ammunition.

 "The District Commissioner and I are quite satisfied with the existing state of affairs, and, when a proper system of police has been established, I do not think there will be any further cause for anxiety.

 "Meantime, I am continuing patrols throughout the district, so far as the number of mounted troops permit of my doing so, and I have route marches twice a week.

 "2. I have the honour to forward report from Captain Henning, 4th Battalion Scottish Rifles, in reference to the duty upon which I sent him on the 31st ult., and referred to in paragraph five of my report of the 3rd June.

 "Captain Henning returned here by a different route, and marched over 100 miles in six and a-half days, and I have been informed that his march had an excellent effect in the district.

 "3. I am glad to report that the sickness among the troops has decreased, but there are still over 100 cases in hospital, and there is not, in my opinion, a proper supply of necessaries and comforts for the sick. I have consulted with the S.M.O. on the subject, and beg to be informed whether the strength of the force at present at Boshof is to be maintained; as, if so, it will be absolutely necessary either to purchase sheets and other requisite articles for the hospital—a cooking-stove amongst the number— or to get a stationary hospital for a hundred beds sent here. And I beg to draw attention most earnestly to this.

 " I have the honour to be,
  " Sir,
   " Your obedient servant,
    "(Sgd.) ARTHUR H. COURTENAY, *Colonel*,
  " *Commanding 3rd and 4th Battalions Scottish Rifles,*
   " *Commandant, Boshof.*"

As will be observed by these reports, the Commandant sent a party under Captain Henning to Quaggashoek, on the 31st May, with the following orders :—

"To Captain HENNING, 4th Battalion Scottish Rifles.

"You will proceed to-morrow, the 31st inst., in command of a mixed force of artillery, with two guns, yeomanry, and infantry, consisting of yourself, 6 officers, and 111 N.C.O.'s and men, with Civil Surgeon Loch, in medical charge, to Walker's Farm, Quaggashoek, about forty miles east of Boshof, with a view to capturing Zarps, or Boers, supposed to be under the command of Van-der-Post, as mentioned in wire from Military Governor, Bloemfontein, to the District Commissioner, Boshof, dated 29th May. A guide will accompany you. You will take every precaution as regards advance guards and scouting, and you will order all under your command to keep a good look-out for any small parties of Boers or Kaffirs. Any without passes should be made prisoners.

"Your infantry are mounted for the purpose of quick transport between this and Quaggashoek, and back here ; and you are at liberty to use some of them for scouting or other necessary purpose that may to you seem advisable, but you will not (unless absolutely certain that it is necessary to do so) proceed beyond Walker's Farm, and, in any case, not farther than ten miles from there, in an opposite direction to Boshof.

"You will return here not later than Wednesday, the 6th

June, unless circumstances arise that, in your opinion, point to the object of your mission not being carried out successfully without one or two days further limit of time, but no longer.

"You will make enquiries also for Commandant Deedrechts, and make him a prisoner if possible.

"(Sgd.) ARTHUR H. COURTENAY, *Colonel*,
"*Commandant, Boshof.*"
"BOSHOF, 30*th May*, 1900."

The following officers accompanied Captain Henning on the expedition :—Lieutenant Nesham, 38th Battery R.F.A.; Lieutenant Viner Johnson, I.Y.; Lieutenants Shaw and Fitzgerald, 3rd Battalion South Wales Borderers; and Captain Burns-Macdonald and Lieutenant Bridgman, 4th Battalion Scottish Rifles.

On arriving at Quaggashoek they advanced upon a kopje some distance off, where the Zarps had been located, but on arriving there found it evacuated. The party returned to Boshof by a different route, and their march had an excellent effect in the district.

A detachment of the 2nd Battalion Scottish Rifles from home, numbering 200 N.C.O.'s and men, joined the 4th Battalion at Boshof on the 11th July.

The Boshof district remained perfectly quiet for some time after this, and the Commandant and officers of the garrison received many invitations to shoot from Burghers in the neighbourhood, and secured some excellent specimens of Wildebeest and Hartebeest, besides Springbok and other game.

CHAPTER II.

(15th May to 16th August, 1900.)

SERVICES OF DETACHMENT WITH THE 20TH BRIGADE, 1ST DIVISION.

IN compliance with orders received from Colonel A. H. Courtenay, Commandant at Boshof, four companies of the battalion joined the 20th Brigade, under Major-General A. H. Paget, C.V.O., late Scots Guards, belonging to the 1st Division, commanded by Lieut.-General Lord Methuen, K.C.V.O., C.B., C.M.G., on the 15th May, on which day it marched out of Boshof. The composition of the Brigade is given in the previous chapter, p. 10. The detachment was under the command of Major and Hon. Lieut.-Colonel Montague Johnstone, who had with him Captain A. F. Townsend, acting Adjutant, Lieutenants M. H. D. Thomson-Carmichael, G. F. Phillips, R. Forbes, and J. D. Anderson.

Between the 15th of May and the 16th of August the detachment of the regiment took part in all the operations in which the 20th Brigade was engaged in the Orange Free State, marching with the Brigade to Hoopstad, Bothaville, Kroonstad, Lindley, Bethlehem, Senekal, Winburg, back to Senekal, and Slabbert's Nek, and back again to Senekal and Winburg.

At Hoopstad Lieutenant Thomson-Carmichael fell ill, and was obliged to remain there until he rejoined Headquarters at Boshof.

The detachment was first under fire on the 3rd June, when *en route* to Lindley, whither the 1st Division had been ordered from Kroonstad to relieve the Irish Yeomanry, who had unfortunately been made prisoners sixteen hours previous to the Advance Guard of the 1st Division arriving there. From the 3rd June to the 3rd July the 20th Brigade was "shut up" at Lindley, and subjected to daily shelling and sniping, also to a heavy attack by the two De Wets with six guns on the 26th June. During this period the detachment of the 4th Scottish Rifles occupied a hill, which they named "Lanark Hill," about one mile east of Lindley. On the 26th June, alone, 200 shells fell or burst over them. On a hill to their left was a half battalion of the 2nd Yorkshire Light Infantry, and on one to their right the 4th Battalion South Staffordshire. At Lindley the detachment lost two men killed and one wounded, their comparative immunity from casualties being chiefly due to the excellent manner in which they entrenched themselves.

While at Lindley early in June, a flag of truce was observed approaching the Examining Guard of the 4th Scottish Rifles, stationed at the foot of "Lanark Hill," and guarding the approach to Lindley from the Bethlehem direction. Lieut.-Colonel Johnstone and Captain Townsend proceeded from the kopje, and found it was General Piet de Wet, whom they gave to understand, through an interpreter (as he could not speak English), that he would have to be blindfolded. To this De Wet objected, saying that it was by the invitation of the British General that he had come to the British lines, in order to make arrangements to stop the war, " and that, if Colonel Johnstone insisted, he must request Lord Methuen to come and meet him outside the British lines or inside those of the Boers." Two Field-Cornets, accompanying De Wet, were blindfolded, and, upon the latter giving his word of honour, as a gentleman, that his only intention in coming in was to do as he had stated, he was allowed to pass.   Lieut.-Colonel Johnstone then proceeded to Headquarters to report, and he was told that he had acted in accordance with the wishes of the General (General Paget, who had been left full instructions by Lord Methuen, when the latter left Boshof with the 9th Brigade). It was well known that this Boer Commander had been for some time anxious to surrender, having several times expressed himself to this effect, and had only been kept from doing so by the Commandants on his own side.   Piet de Wet subsequently surrendered at Kroonstad, towards the end of July, 1900 ; not, however, before causing the brigade a deal of annoyance, in conjunction with his elder brother Christian de Wet, Prinsloo, and other Boer leaders.   The result of the interview between General Paget and Piet de Wet was that there was to be a five days' armistice. Considerable surprise, however, was felt by the troops at Lindley when only forty-eight hours had elapsed and a heavy fire was opened by the Boer guns, the reason afterwards given being, that President Steyn, who was then at Vrede, said that De Wet had no authority to conclude an armistice, and that the shelling must therefore continue.

From Lindley, on the 3rd July, in company with Clements' Brigade, the 20th Brigade (including the 4th Scottish Rifles) marched on Bethlehem, having heavy fighting at

Leeuwkop, where the 4th Scottish Rifles acted as escort to
the C.I.V. guns. On the 5th July the Brigade arrived
outside Bethlehem, and the enemy started shelling at dawn
the following morning. That day, half the detachment
4th Scottish Rifles was engaged holding a ridge, and was
shelled at long range until relieved by the 2nd Battalion
Wiltshire Regiment.

The following day, 7th July, the Boers opened fire at
dawn, principally on the 2nd Yorkshire Light Infantry and
the 4th Scottish Rifles, who were holding a ridge until the
enemy were obliged to withdraw their guns, our lyddite guns
having silenced them. On this day, 2nd Lieutenant
H. Boyd-Rochfort was amongst those wounded, and the
1st Battalion Royal Irish Regiment lost four officers and
46 men ; the total casualties being about 130. On the
8th July the detachment took over another ridge outside
Bethlehem and fortified it, and held it until the morning of
the 15th July, when, on being relieved by the 2nd Battalion
Seaforth Highlanders, they marched with their own Brigade
and Broadwood's Cavalry Brigade to intercept C. de Wet.
On the 16th July the detachment formed the right flank
guard to the convoy, when the column came in touch with
C. de Wet's force, which included five guns. The enemy
advanced against the right flank, but were met with a well-
directed fire from the 4th Battalion Scottish Rifles, who
kept them at bay until the entire convoy had passed, the
enemy being within 400 yards when the last man of the
detachment moved off.

The detachment was then detailed as part of an escort to
take an empty convoy to Winburg for supplies, and arrived
there without any important incident on the 21st July.

They left Winburg on the 23rd July with a convoy nearly six miles long, arriving at Slabbert's Nek without any incident except sniping by the enemy.

The detachment assisted in holding Slabbert's Nek, to prevent the escape of the enemy on the important occasion when Prinsloo's Commando was obliged to surrender to General Paget; and on the 4th August the 20th Brigade, with the detachment of the Regiment, started from Slabbert's Nek for Winburg with 2252 prisoners of war, including the Ladybrand, Ficksburg, Senekal, Bethlehem, Wepener, Rouxville, and Thabanchu Commandos, the last two named being in charge of the 4th Battalion Scottish Rifles. Winburg was reached on the 9th August.

On the 10th August half the detachment of the 4th Scottish Rifles left Winburg by train for Cape Town, in charge of 592 prisoners of war; the remainder of the detachment following the next day with an equal number of prisoners. At Naaouwpoort Junction, Cape Colony, the detachment handed over the prisoners to the 4th Battalion Royal Lancaster Regiment for conveyance to Cape Town, having received orders to proceed to Kimberley *en route* to Boshof to join Headquarters, which was reached by march-route from Kimberley, on the 16th August.

During the three months' operations above referred to, the detachment of the 4th Scottish Rifles must have marched about 600 miles, and, in common with the rest of the troops engaged, suffered great hardships, especially in the very cold weather at night, when the want of warm clothing and boots was very much felt.

On arrival at Winburg, the 4th Scottish Rifles were practically in rags, but they were there re-equipped. Writing to Colonel Courtenay, Major-General A. Paget expresses his appreciation of the services of the detachment as follows :—

"EAST OF WATERVAL, 3rd *October*, 1900.

" MY DEAR COURTENAY,—I want, in the first place, to apologise for not having written to you before, to thank you for the great services rendered to my column by the 200 men you sent me under Colonel Johnstone.

" I have been incessantly and constantly on the move since I left Lindley, and it will always be a source of regret that I was unable to say a few words of farewell and thanks to Colonel Johnstone and his officers, N.C.O.'s, and men with him. You can well imagine that on arriving at a place with a huge convoy of prisoners that I had to cater for, with an order to at once entrain my force, to take over a new regiment, and to exchange two squadrons yeomanry with two squadrons of volunteers, my time was not my own.

" You will tell Colonel Johnstone that I made special mention of himself and his men in my despatch, and also by word of mouth to the Chief, and that I consider the steadiness and pluck shown by your men through a trying fortnight at Lindley worthy of the greatest praise. They were subjected to a continuous and heavy shell-fire, enough to shake the nerves of any but the best troops ; but from what I could see, your officers and men seemed quite in their element, and to enjoy the excitement and danger.

" I was sorry that you were (that you had to be) left behind, or you would certainly have had your chance of leading your battalion to victory at Bethlehem. I am also glad to be able to tell you that the general good conduct of your men was excellent, they gave me no trouble, and their marching was also worthy of the greatest praise.

" My only regret was, and is, that there were not more of them. I trust that they have not suffered in health, I know that a great many were invalided.

" Please remember me to Colonel Johnstone, and thank him for his letter, and believe me,

" Always sincerely yours,
" (Sgd.) ARTHUR PAGET.

" *P.S.*—Pray remember my address, 35 Belgrave Square, and come and see me if ever we return home."

CHAPTER III.

(15th *August* 1900 *to* 23rd *May* 1901.)

Operations around Boshof—Investment of Boshof.

THE detachment of the 4th Scottish Rifles which had been with the 20th Brigade rejoined Headquarters at Boshof on the 15th August. Lieut.-Colonel Montague Johnstone took over command of the battalion from Major Chavasse a few weeks later, having remained at Kimberley for a short leave *en route* to Boshof. Captain A. F. Townsend resumed his duties of Staff-Officer in place of Captain J. Campbell Gardner, who was appointed to command the Mounted Infantry raised in the 4th Scottish Rifles. These latter had been commanded in the first instance by Captain D. Burns-Macdonald who took a great interest in them, and did a good deal of patrolling in the district until he was obliged to go home on sick leave early in September.

Between the middle of July and September the garrison of Boshof was considerably reduced. The half Battalion of the 3rd South Wales Borderers had gone to Warrenton and Fourteen Streams under Lieut.-Colonel Healy, while nearly all the details of the 1st Division had rejoined their respective battalions, so that the garrison numbered little over 900.

Colonel Courtenay being obliged to proceed to Cape Town

on sick leave on the 6th September, Lieut.-Colonel Montague Johnstone took over the duties of Commandant of Boshof, and Major Chavasse, those of Officer Commanding the 4th Scottish Rifles, until Colonel Courtenay's return to Boshof on the 25th September.

On the 9th September two farmers arrived from the north of the district and reported that they had been commandeered on the 7th, and had come to Boshof, having been cut off from Hoopstad by the enemy's patrols. On the same day Captain J. Campbell Gardner and some of the Mounted Infantry section of the 4th Scottish Rifles were sent to Karreepan, about thirty miles north of Boshof, to patrol the district and reassure the farmers. At 7.30 same evening a wire having been received from Christiana that a patrol of the enemy was at Karreepan, Lieutenant Viner Johnson and twenty-one men of the Imperial Yeomanry were sent there to reinforce Captain Gardner. On the 11th, Lieutenant Brudenell Murphy and the remainder of the Mounted Infantry Section 4th Scottish Rifles were sent north with orders to join Captain Gardner's party. Captain Gardner and his party came in contact with the enemy near the Vaal at daybreak on the 14th, and had one man wounded, and retired on Roodepoort Farm (the property of Mr. Mooy, a Belgian, who was thoroughly in sympathy with and loyal to the British), which he fortified. He was attacked there by a large party of the enemy on the 15th, and drove them off. He then proceeded to Christiania, where he arrived on the 19th, having taken Mr. and Mrs. Mooy there for safety, subsequently returning to Boshof. Captain Lynch, who had been attached to the 1st Battalion Royal Munster Fusiliers with the 20th Brigade since May, and had seen a great deal

D

of service with them in the Orange Free State and Transvaal, returned to Headquarters on the 15th September.

After this the district became more and more disturbed. Parties of the enemy came from the Transvaal and north of the Orange River Colony, and partly by persuasion and partly by terrorising the inhabitants, induced many of them to break their oath and go again on "Commando."

The Commandant, whose mounted force at this time did not exceed sixty, including the Mounted Infantry raised in the 4th Scottish Rifles, made frequent application for more mounted troops; but it was not found possible to accede to his application, and he received orders from Major-General Settle, D.S.O., R.E., not to patrol the district at any great distance from Boshof, not having sufficient mounted troops at his disposal for the purpose. From the middle of October onwards frequent reports were received of Boer patrols in the district, and the sending of convoys to Hoopstad with supplies from Boshof (which had been proceeding since its occupation by the 1st Division in May) became a matter of great danger.

Boshof was less fortunate than many other commands in the number of its mounted troops. It was quite impossible to properly police the district, or afford due protection to those Boers who had surrendered and taken the oath of neutrality; and to this cause much of the trouble which subsequently occurred is due. Those who surrendered, and had given up their arms, and taken the oath of allegiance or neutrality, ought to have been sent away from their districts as prisoners of war in the first instance. It was impossible in a district about the size of Wales to afford proper protection with the small mounted force at

Boshof.   The result was that 75 per cent. of those who surrendered to the Commandant at Boshof in May and June, 1900, must have subsequently broken their oaths and gone again on "Commando"; some, no doubt, willingly, but the majority under compulsion.

A post was established at Graspan about twenty-four miles north of Boshof, on the road to Hoopstad, consisting of Lieutenant Faulkener, with twenty-five men and two guns, Diamond Fields Artillery; Lieutenants Glossop and Maxwell-Heron, with seventy-five N.C.O.'s and men, 4th Scottish Rifles; and Lieutenant Brudenell Murphy, and eight men of the Mounted Infantry Section 4th Scottish Rifles; the whole under Captain Littledale, 4th Scottish Rifles.

While at Graspan the detachment was surrounded by the enemy, but having entrenched themselves well, they were not subjected to any attacks.

Lieutenant Brudenell Murphy and one of the Mounted Infantry were taken prisoners by the enemy on the 17th October when out patrolling, having gone too near a farmhouse, which they did not think held any of the enemy. They were, however, released the same day by the Boer Commandant, C. Badenhorst, and sent back on foot to Graspan, about eight miles, their horses, rifles, and ammunition being kept by the enemy.

The detachment at Graspan returned to Boshof with Major-General Settle's Column, which passed Graspan *en route* from Hoopstad, and arrived at Boshof on the 30th October, after which date no convoy was able to proceed to Hoopstad from Boshof.

On the 21st October a small party of the Orange River

Colony Police, having been sent to make some arrests about twenty miles east of Boshof, under Lieutenant Russell, 4th Scottish Rifles, were attacked by a largely superior force of the enemy at the farm of Daamplaats. One of the Police was taken prisoner, and the rest retired to Boshof, their retreat being covered by a party from the latter place under the Commandant.

Captain Kemp and thirty-five men of the 23rd Company, Imperial Yeomanry, with two Colt guns, arrived at Boshof from Kimberley on the 24th October, to reinforce the mounted troops. They would at the time have been a great acquisition in assisting to clear the district, but were recalled by wire to Kimberley the following day.

On the 26th October Colonel Courtenay (having heard by wire of the treacherous conduct of some of the inhabitants of Jacobsdal in firing on the British troops, when an attack was made on that place by the Boers) ordered all the male inhabitants of Boshof to sleep under Guard in the Dutch Reformed Church, where he subsequently detained any of whom he had any suspicion by day as well.

At this time those in authority in South Africa were under the happy delusion that the war was practically at an end by the formal annexation of the South African Republic on the 25th of October. Indeed, very shortly afterwards, Lord Roberts started for home, leaving Lord Kitchener, just to wind up affairs, as it were. But we had a deal to learn and a deal to do, and more reverses to suffer, before the Boers were subdued. In the meantime there was to be more self-sacrifice on the part of officers, and more of that firm and enduring courage on the part of the uncomplaining British soldier, whether regular, militiaman, yeoman, volunteer, or colonial.

On the 28th October, the camp of the 4th Scottish Rifles in Boshof was broken up, and the men were ordered to occupy the ground in the rear of their own trenches round the town, while two companies were ordered to occupy strongly entrenched positions at the Green and West Kopjes. General Settle's Column which, as already stated, arrived at Boshof on the 30th October, left for Kimberley ; the first portion, under Colonel Sir C. Parsons, on the 31st October, and the remainder, under General Settle, on the 1st November.*

Late on the evening of 1st November an urgent message came into Boshof from a non-commissioned officer in charge of a steam convoy coming from Kimberley, to the effect that a large party of the enemy were in the neighbourhood of Leeuwfontein, and asking for reinforcements. Captain J. Campbell Gardner, Lieutenants Russell and Brudenell Murphy, 4th Scottish Rifles, and Lieutenant Viner Johnson, I.Y., with all available mounted men of the Scottish Rifles and Imperial Yeomanry, were at once despatched to Leeuwfontein, and were reinforced next morning by 100 men, 4th Scottish Rifles, and two guns of the Diamond Fields Artillery, under Captain A. F. Townsend, Lieutenant Bridgman, 4th Scottish Rifles, and Lieutenant Faulkener, Diamond Fields Artillery, the whole under Captain Henning, 4th Scottish Rifles. The steam convoy, which was in danger of being captured, was brought in in safety.

On the 4th November, Captain J. Campbell Gardner was sent out with all available mounted troops, and Lieutenants

---

* Captain Protheroe Smith, who had had an attack of scarlatina, left for home on sick leave.

Russell and Brudenell Murphy, 4th Scottish Rifles, and Viner Johnson, I.Y., to the farm of Blauwboschfontein, about twelve miles east of Boshof.

Leaving Boshof at 2 A.M., they reached the farm before daybreak, and rescued two burghers (who had been commandeered the day previous by a large commando, which had been at this and neighbouring farms for the purpose of commandeering), and made prisoners of two armed Boers who had been left in charge.

During November frequent skirmishes took place between the mounted troops at Boshof and the enemy when the former were out patrolling, and the latter increased daily in numbers, and began cutting the telegraph wire between Boshof and Kimberley.

On the 22nd November, the mail-cart from Windsorton Road Station (which carried the mails between that place and Boshof three times a-week) was held up by the enemy at Rietvlei, about twelve miles north-west of Boshof. Nursing Sister Constance Fullagar, who was the only occupant of the mail-cart except the driver, and who was *en route* from Kimberley to Boshof to attend a serious case of enteric, was compelled to leave the cart and to walk some distance to a neighbouring farm, where she was lent a cart to proceed to Boshof. The Boers who held up the mail-cart were very rude to her, and they seized the mails and everything else in the cart, including the native driver.

After this date (22nd November) the Commandant ordered all the men of his garrison to sleep in their trenches, as Boshof became practically invested by two commandos*—namely, those of Jacobs and C. Badenhorst.

---

* The former known as "De Wet's Verkenning Korps."

On the 29th November at 9.15 P.M. the enemy attacked the town in force, opening a very heavy rifle fire on the south side, to which the outposts replied with volleys. A large number of the enemy's bullets fell all over the town, and created much alarm among the female population (most of the Dutch males were, as already stated, in the church, where they could do no harm!). The trenches were manned immediately, and the enemy, who continued the attack for a considerable time on the south-east of the town, were subsequently driven off, not having succeeded in getting nearer than 500 yards.

Captain Blaikie-Hislop and one man, 4th Scottish Rifles, were slightly wounded, and it was, no doubt, owing to the depth of the trenches, and the excellence of the head cover, that there were not many more casualties. The enemy were reported to have had several casualties, and to have sent a cart during the night to remove their wounded.

On the 28th November, a "White Flag" arrived from the enemy, with a letter from Commandant Jacobs, of which the following is a copy and translation :—

> "HOOFD. KOMDT. DE WET'S VERKENNINGS KORPS,
> "ONDER KAPITAN JACOBS.
> "JEN VELDE, 29 *Nov.*, 1900.

" Den Bevelvoerende Officier,
" Harer Majesteits der Britsche Ryks Macht, Boshof.

"WEL ED HEER,—Op last van Hoofd. Komdt. C. R. de Wet worat ued verzocht alle vrouwen en kinderen toe te laten het dorp Boshof te verlaten voor morgen avond ten zes uur (den 30 Nov.). Wij vertrouwen dat ued als een-eerlijk man met een menschelijk hait niet toe laten zal dat de nie in Boshof macht van het Britsche Reguring schulen zal achter het onschuldig bloed van vrouwen en kinderen : zoo zur wij met verwachting af het uittrek van alle vrouwen en kinderen uit Boshof.

"Jen bewijs onzer beschaving zijn wij nochtans gereid met ued persoonlijk onder handelingen aan te gaan en ziju wij ter uwer beschekking om ued te ont moeten ten huize van den Heer Schijf (tijd door ued te worden bepaald).

"Daar wij een beschaafd oorlog voeren wordt ued vriende lijk verzocht onze rapport rijder met witte vlag zonder verzuim terug te zenden en zoo onze witte vlag te respecteeren.

"By order,

"(Sgd.) J. Bosman,

"*Wd. Assist. Landdrost, Bothaville,*

"*Dt. Kroonstad.*"

Translation.

"Chief Commandant de Wet's Scouting Corps,

"Under Captain Jacobs.

"The Veldt, 29th *November,* 1900.

"*To the Officer Commanding*

"*Her Britannic Majesty's Forces, Boshof.*

"Honoured Sir,—By order of General C. R. de Wet, you are hereby requested to allow all the women and children to leave the town of Boshof before six o'clock to-morrow evening, the 30th November.

"We trust that you, as a man of honour, and with a manly heart, will not allow that the force in Boshof of the British Government should shelter behind the innocent blood of women and children. Therefore we shall expect with confidence the exit of all women and children from Boshof.

"We are at the same time willing to treat with you personally, and would go to meet and talk with you at Mr. Scaife's house at any time fixed by you.

"As we are waging a civilised war, you are kindly requested to send back our despatch rider (with white flag) without hurt, and thus to respect our white flag.

"By order,

"(Signed) J. Bosman,

"*Asst. Landdrost, Bothaville,*

"*Dist. Kroonstad.*"

The Commandant sent his staff-officer (Captain A. F. Townsend) to meet Commandant Jacobs the following day at Scaife's farm, about four miles south of Boshof, to inform him that he had no intention whatever of complying with his request.

Commandant Jacobs and his secretary Bosman then demanded the surrender of the town (with the condition that the British troops on laying down their arms should have safe conduct to Kimberley), or, in the alternative, that the women and children in the town should be sent out and kept in a safe place by the British.

Captain Townsend informed them that neither of these propositions could be entertained, and pointed out that the continuance of the war was ruining their country, and that they should accept the inevitable and surrender, to which they replied, that if it took seven years to drive the British out, they were prepared to again develop the country as they had done before, and that they would fight to the end. Captain Townsend handed to Commandant Jacobs copies of Lord Roberts' recent proclamations, and the interview ended.

After this date Boshof became more closely invested by the enemy, whose numbers increased considerably. No letters were received from or sent to Kimberley except by despatch riders, and for several weeks no letters from home were received. Two despatch riders with two scouts were captured by the enemy when returning from Kimberley, and were shot in cold blood.

The telegraph wire to Kimberley which had been cut by the enemy on six different occasions since the beginning of November, and had been repaired on each occasion by troops from Boshof, was finally destroyed for a distance of five miles, and it became impossible to repair it again.

About this time, owing to the reduction of the Garrision, and the closer proximity of the enemy, it became necessary to make alterations and improvements in the defences of the town. A very strong redoubt was constructed round the church square, while the external defences were considerably strengthened and improved by wire entanglements, &c.

A convoy arrived at Boshof on the 15th December, escorted by a column under Colonel Parke. On the previous day the kopjes and ridges round and near Leeuwfontein had been occupied and held by all the available troops from Boshof. Colonel Courtenay, Captain Townsend, and some of the Scottish Rifles Mounted Infantry proceeded to Leeuwfontein to meet the column, and took part in an engagement at the farm of Viljoens Hoef, which was captured and burned, the enemy having continued to fire on our troops after they (the enemy) had hoisted a white flag.

There were several casualties, and a portion of the force, including the Hampshire Yeomanry, subsequently proceeded under Colonel Courtenay to Reitfontein, Pretorious' farm, which was taken without furthur opposition. The column and empty convoy returned to Kimberley on the 16th December, taking with them 100 N.C.O.'s and men of the 4th Scottish Rifles under Captain Mellish and Lieutenant Seagrim. From this date the Kimberley Flying Column had two officers and 100 N.C.O.'s and men of the battalion with them throughout all their operations, until the battalion left for home at the end of May, 1901.

The Garrison of Boshof was thus further reduced to about 800 of all ranks. Captain T. K. Gardner rejoined the battalion from the Northumberland Fusiliers, with which he had served continuously in all the operations of the 9th Brigade since May, 1900.

On the 20th December a foraging party went out with two guns, under Captain Devenish, R.F.A., who had with him Captain Lynch and Lieutenant Brudenell Murphy, 4th Scottish Rifles, and Lieutenant Viner Johnson, I.Y., with all available Mounted Infantry and Yeomanry, also fifty N.C.O.'s and men, 4th Scottish Rifles, under Lieutenant Hazlerigg as escort for the guns.

They found Boschrand ridge occupied in force by the enemy, and the guns coming into action, the enemy vacated the position pursued by the Imperial Yeomanry and Mounted Infantry of the 4th Scottish Rifles, who were not, however, strong enough to continue the pursuit.* The casualties were one man, Scottish Rifles, and one man, Imperial Yeomanry, wounded, the latter dangerously. On this occasion the Commandant brought to the notice of the Commander-in-Chief the gallant conduct of Colour-Sergeant A. E. Slade of the 4th Scottish Rifles, acting Sergeant-Major of the Mounted Infantry Section, who, when only 200 yards from Boschrand ridge, which was occupied by the enemy, returned on his horse, after his men had been ordered to retire, and under a very heavy fire picked up Lance-Corporal Whittingham, 2nd Battalion Scottish Rifles, attached to 4th Scottish Rifles, M.I., who was lying wounded on the veldt, and carried him on his own horse to join the rest of his party.

On the 27th December a foraging party was sent out

---

* For an account of these operations, see Chapter IV.

under Captain Henning, with whom were Captain Devenish and two guns, 44th Battery R.F.A., all available yeomanry and mounted infantry under Lieutenant Johnson, I.Y., and Lieutenant Brudenell Murphy, 4th Scottish Rifles, and 100 N.C.O.'s and men 4th Scottish Rifles, under Captains Clifford and Lynch. They visited the farms of Reitfontein (Pretorious') and Tweefontein (Van Wijk's) and brought in 100 cattle, 34 horses ,500 sheep, and 1700 lbs. of forage. They also brought in Van Wijk as a prisoner, as he was reported to have been implicated in the shooting of the despatch riders and scouts before referred to. The party met with no opposition.

On the 29th December, all available mounted troops under Lieutenants Johnson and Brudenell Murphy, with two guns, 44th Battery R.F.A., under Captain Devenish, and 50 of the 4th Scottish Rifles, the whole under the Commandant with his S.O., proceeded to the farm of Kalkfontein, and brought in 1900 lbs. of oat-hay, seven head of cattle, and two horses.

About 100 of the enemy were reported on a neighbouring ridge, but did not come within range. On the same day at noon there was a very heavy thunderstorm, and Private Douglas, " D " Company, 4th Scottish Rifles, was killed by lightning when on duty at the west kopje.

On 4th January, 1901, all available mounted men under Lieutenants Johnson and Brudenell Murphy, with two guns Diamond Fields Artillery, under Captain Devenish, and 100 men of the 4th Scottish Rifles under Captain Blake and Lieutenant Glossop, proceeded with the Commandant and his S.O. to the farm of Rabenthal, about nine miles from

Boshof, and brought in 1000 sheep, 100 horses and cattle, three wagon-loads of forage, and two prisoners. The party was unopposed, although a large force of the enemy was reported by the scouts on an adjoining farm. On the same day a sick convoy proceeded to Kimberley under Lieutenant Dinnis, R.A.M.C., 2nd Lieutenant Boyd-Rochfort, who was convalescent from scarlet fever, proceeded to Kimberley with this convoy *en route* to Cape Town.

On the 5th January, the scouts having been fired on from Boschrand Ridge at 10 A.M., all available mounted men under Lieutenants Johnson and Brudenell Murphy went out, supported by two guns, R.F.A., under Captain Devenish, and 100 4th Scottish Rifles under Captain Clifford, the whole under the Commandant and his S.O. The enemy were shelled off Boschrand Kopje and driven off a ridge by rifle fire. The yeomanry advanced on the left, and the Scottish Rifles Mounted Infantry, with some attached mounted men of the Diamond Fields Artillery, on the right, and the latter were heavily engaged for some time. The party returned to Boshof at 3.30 P.M. Casualties, one man, D.F.A., and one horse, 4th Scottish Rifles Mounted Infantry, wounded. The enemy were reported to have had several casualties.

On the 7th January, an ambulance returning from Kimberley with Lieutenants Dinnis, R.A.M.C., and orderlies, under the Red Cross, was captured by the enemy near Boschrand. Lieutenant Dinnis and his orderly were made prisoners and were sent back next day to Kimberley, all the medical and other comforts were seized by the enemy. The following day the Commandant sent out his S.O., under White Flag, to expostulate at this conduct.

Captain Townsend met some of the enemy's scouts a few miles out and rode with them towards the laager, but was not permitted to go with them all the way. They returned, however to Captain Townsend, and stated that their Commandant was away, but that he would meet Colonel Courtenay at Boschrand on the next day but one, and accordingly the Commandant and his S.O. met Commandants Jacobs and Bosman on the 10th, and remonstrated with them on the capture of the ambulance and medical comforts. The former they refused to give up, but agreed to return the medical comforts they had seized, if sent for to a neighbouring farm, and this was accordingly done, Captain Blaikie-Hislop and a party being detailed for the purpose.

On the 8th January, at 8.30 A.M., a party of the enemy galloped in to within 600 yards of the town on the north side, and having made prisoners of one N.C.O. and five men of the Imperial Yeomanry, who formed part of the cattle guard, but were apparently not on the alert, succeeded in driving off some of the cattle. As soon as observed the enemy were fired upon and shelled, and retired hastily, their casualties being unknown.

Skirmishes of minor importance took place daily until the 17th January, upon which date a despatch rider arrived from Colonel Milne, D.S.O., commanding the Kimberley Column, stating that he was at Slabbert's Farm with a convoy *en route* to Boshof, where he expected to arrive the following morning, and asking to be supported by the troops at Boshof. Accordingly, during the afternoon the scouts were sent out under Captain Blaikie-Hislop, and found Boschrand occupied by the enemy's scouts, whom they drove off after a sharp fight. On occupying Boschrand they saw a large party of the enemy advancing towards the neighbouring kopjes, and Captain Blaikie-Hislop sent back for reinforcements. All available Mounted Infantry and Yeomanry at once proceeded out with the Commandant and S.O., and occupied Boschrand and neighbouring kopjes, just in time to prevent the enemy from doing so. They were relieved later by 125 of the 4th Scottish Rifles under Captain J. Campbell Gardner, and Lieutenants Hazlerigg and Bridgman, who held four kopjes overlooking Leeuwfontein the whole night. On the following morning, at 4 A.M., two guns R.F.A., under Captain Devenish, escorted by the Yeomanry and Mounted Infantry, proceeded to one of the ridges held by the infantry during the previous night. During the morning a large number of the enemy were seen, and the guns of the approaching Column were heard in action. The Column and convoy arrived at Leeuwfontein at 5 P.M., having been very heavily engaged, and after a halt proceeded to Boshof, leaving, however, seven steam transport trains at Leeuwfontein, which necessitated the party from Boshof holding the kopjes for a second night. On this occasion the 100 men of the Scottish Rifles (under Captain Mellish and Lieutenant Seagrim), who were with the Kimberley Column, charged, and under a very heavy fire took a kopje held by the enemy, three of the Scottish Rifles being wounded. The Assistant Inspector-General, Kimberley Section, sent the following order to the Commandant :—

" To Colonel COURTENAY,
        "*Commandant, Boshof.*

" The A.I.G. desires me to inform you that he has read the report of the 27th January, 1901, with interest. He congratulates you and the Garrison of Boshof on their work on 18th January, which resulted in a decided advantage to the British side, and in the death of a Boer leader, Stoeffel Lotz.

"By Order,
"(Sgd.) R. J. STUART, *Major*,
"*C.S.O., Kimberley Section.*"

On the 19th January the steam transport of Colonel Milne's Column arrived about 7 A.M. from Leeuwfontein, with their own escort, and the men of the Scottish Rifles, who had held the kopjes during the night. The enemy harassed the rearguard coming in, but there were no casualties. At 5 P.M. same day Dennison's Scouts, supported by two guns R.F.A., under Lieutenant Mundy, and 125 of the 4th Scottish Rifles, under Captain T. K. Gardner, Lieutenants Thomson-Carmichael and Bridgman, proceeded to take the ridges between Boshof and Leeuwfontein, which were again held by the enemy, who were driven out after a skirmish.

On the 20th, Colonel Milne's Column and empty convoy left Boshof for Kimberley, being accompanied to Leeuwfontein by the mounted troops and two guns from Boshof. On this occasion Captain Blake took over command of the detachment 4th Scottish Rifles with the Kimberley Column from Captain Mellish. The Commandant sent 79 undesirables (males) and 45 natives to Kimberley with the Column.

Nothing of any importance except skirmishes between scouts of both sides occurred until the 26th, on which date, at 4 A.M., all available mounted troops, under Lieutenants Viner Johnson and Brudenell Murphy, supported by two guns R.F.A., under Lieutenant Mundy, and 120 Scottish Rifles under Captain Henning and Lieutenants Maxwell-Heron and Anderson, proceeded to Roux's Farm, which had for some weeks been a rendezvous for Boer patrols. The Commandant and Staff-Officer accompanied the party, which brought into Boshof Roux and his family, 108 horses, and over 300 goats. The mounted portion of the force attempted to go on to Combrink's Farm, Swartfontein, but were fired upon by a much superior force of the enemy from the ridges over-looking the farm, and were obliged to retire.

On the 27th two despatch riders arrived from Kimberley, bringing the sad news of the death of Her Majesty Queen Victoria.

Up to the 2nd February there were daily skirmishes with parties of the enemy, who, on several occasions, had to be shelled off Merriesfontein Ridge, about three miles from the town.

On the 2nd February a wood-cutting party, consisting of all available mounted men under Lieutenants Johnson and Brudenell Murphy, 100 of the 4th Scottish Rifles, with machine gun and wagons, proceeded, under Captain Henning (who had with him Captain Clifford and Lieu-tenants Bridgman, Anderson, and Maxwell-Heron), to Merriesfontein Ridge.   Private Harris, 1st Northumberland Fusiliers, who was one of the scouts in advance of the party, was ambushed and shot dead by the enemy's scouts.   The party returned in the afternoon with over 30,000 lbs. of firewood.

On the 4th February (acting on a cypher despatch received the previous day from Kimberley, with orders to watch Badenhorst's Commando, and to co-operate with the Kimber-ley Column, should they advance north from Paardeberg Drift), a party consisting of all available mounted men, with two guns D.F.A., under the command of Major May, D.F.A., and 125 4th Scottish Rifles, under Captain Henning,

E

with Captains Clifford and Mellish, and Lieutenants Thomson-Carmichael, Anderson, and Maxwell-Heron, proceeded about eight miles to the south and south-west, and made a reconnaissance, visiting the farms Tweefontein and Olivierfontein, owned by H. Jacobs (a prisoner of war) and Van Wijk (on commando) respectively, but found both deserted. About eighty of the enemy were seen in the distance, but did not come within range.

On the 6th February, the Commandant ordered a reconnaissance in force to ascertain, if possible, the exact whereabouts of Badenhorst's and other Commandos in the neighbourhood, the scouts having found it impossible for some time to get out more than three or four miles. All troops available for the purpose were employed, consisting of about 50 Imperial Yeomanry and Mounted Infantry, under Lieutenants Viner Johnson and Brudenell Murphy respectively; 1 section D.F.A., under Major May, D.F.A.; and 100 4th Battalion Scottish Rifles with machine gun, under Captains Henning and Clifford, and Lieutenants G. Hazlerigg, Glossop, Anderson, and Maxwell-Heron, the latter in charge of the Maxim, also some native scouts under Mr. Whitebeard of the Intelligence Department. The orders issued by the Commandant were as follows :—

"To leave Boshof at 4 A.M., thoroughly scout Merriesfontein Ridge, and hold same with infantry at its farther point from Boshof (about four miles), to proceed thence to Kaalplaats Farm, about eight miles south-east, clear same of all stock and food-stuffs, and proceed thence through the open veldt to Eickenboom Farm, five miles north-east of Kaalplaats, clear same and return thence westward to Duivenfontein Farm, about four miles, clear same and return to Boshof."

The infantry were carried in mule wagons from

Merriesfontein, where 50 infantry under Captain Clifford and Lieutenant Glossop were left to hold the ridge. The scouts found some of the enemy's scouts on Merriesfontein, and drove them off after exchanging some shots, Mr. Whitebeard reporting the enemy's scouts to have gone in different directions. The force then proceeded to Kaalplaats, which was found unoccupied, and all stock driven away, the owner (one Uys) having broken his oath and gone again on commando. On leaving Kaalplaats, the guns and infantry, and a few of the mounted men, acting as scouts, proceeded in the direction of Eickenboom, while the remainder of the mounted men under Lieutenants Viner Johnson and Brudenell Murphy made a detour to the right of the farm of Waterberg (about two and a-half miles N.E. of Kaalplaats). Here they heard that there were about 1500 cattle and sheep, and 300 horses, about three miles to their right. Lieutenant Viner Johnson decided to round these up, but while doing so, a large party of Boers opened fire on his party from an adjoining ridge, stampeding the horses which had been collected on the farm. The Mounted Infantry then commenced retiring with the captured cattle, but had not proceeded far when they were attacked by two distinct parties of Boers, who advanced in large numbers from ridges on the right and rear. Having been engaged with these two parties for some time, and holding them in check, the Mounted Infantry eventually met the infantry and guns retiring from Eickenboom. The latter had, in the meantime, proceeded to that farm, upon approaching which, fire was opened upon them by the enemy from the ridges to the left rear of the farm. The guns shelled the enemy, and after a few shots firing ceased, and the farm was occupied by our troops. It had evidently been only very recently evacuated by a large body of the enemy.

While at the farm the ridge commanding it was held by Lieutenant G. Hazlerigg and forty men. That officer observed a large party of the enemy apparently attempting to get between the guns and Merriesfontein Ridge, and opened fire on them, sending a report to Captain Henning, who was at the farm, and who decided to fall back upon Merriesfontein Ridge. While proceeding to do so his party met the Yeomanry and Mounted Infantry, as before narrated, and while falling back on Merriesfontein, the whole were again attacked by a large force of the enemy, on both flanks and in rear. Things at this point looked critical, and a small party of the Mounted Infantry, holding a small ridge, were nearly cut off, but (with the exception of two, whose horses were killed or wounded, and who were made prisoners) managed to escape. The guns and Maxim getting into action with good effect, the enemy withdrew to some extent, and the whole force retired on Merriesfontein in excellent order, the mounted troops keeping up a brisk rearguard engagement the whole way. On this occasion the force engaged, numbering about 130, were opposed by between 300 and 400 of the enemy, the scouts being of opinion that the latter number was more nearly correct.

During the engagement, which lasted over five hours, all ranks of the force acted with the greatest courage and coolness under a most trying and severe fire. Our casualties were as follows:—4th Scottish Rifles Mounted Infantry, Lieutenant R. Brudenell Murphy, and one man wounded, two men taken prisoners; Imperial Yeomanry, three men wounded; Infantry, 4th Scottish Rifles, one man wounded; horses killed or wounded, seventeen. The loss of the enemy amounted to two killed and several wounded. The Commandant and S.O. rode out to Merriesfontein during the morning and witnessed the latter part of the engagement, subsequently accompanying the force back to Boshof.

At a Kaffir hut near Kaalplaats, Mr. Whitebeard ascertained from a Kaffir woman (whose husband was with Badenhorst's Commando) that the latter had returned from Modder River on the previous Tuesday with a large body of men. Lieutenant Brudenell Murphy's conduct throughout the day was most gallant, and his escape was a miraculous one. He had purchased a tame meerkat at Kaalplaats, and had put it in his left breast-pocket. A bullet shortly afterwards struck and killed the meerkat, and being thus diverted, passed down the front of his body, wounding him in two places. Shortly afterwards another bullet struck him on the thigh, but was diverted by a silver medallion and a sovereign, which were in his breeches' pocket, and passed out through the latter, the medallion and sovereign being bent almost double. Lieutenant Murphy continued in command of his men to the end of the day, though he had lost a considerable quantity of blood, and was very weak therefrom. Sergeant G. Fraser, 4th Battalion Scottish Rifles, M.I., also acted with great gallantry, having, under a very heavy fire, bound up Trooper Townshend's, I.Y., wounds (which were very severe and through both lungs) with his puttee, and carried him out of action on his own horse.

The engagement demonstrated the impossibility of operating against the enemy, at any distance exceeding three or four miles from Boshof, with such a small number of mounted troops (about fifty) as were at the disposal of the Commandant. It was clear that infantry, even if carried in wagons, could not hope to cope with men mounted on good horses, and were only useful as escort to guns, and even then hampered the progress of the guns of the advancing force, and still more so of a retiring one.

On the 8th February, the two men who were captured by the enemy during the engagement on the 6th, returned to Boshof, having been released by Badenhorst. They were accompanied by a civilian named Rosser, who had also been taken prisoner by Badenhorst some days previously near Modder River, and brought with them letters from Commandant Badenhorst, and his Adjutant and Secretary, one Schuytze, of which the following are copies :—

" *On Service.*

" DISTRICT—BOSHOF, 7/2/1901.

" Right Honourable Sir Colonel COURTENAY,
    " *Commandant, Boshof.*

" RIGHT HONOURABLE SIR,—Hereby take notice of enclosed Proclamation of the Most Honourable Head Commandant, C. R. de Wet.
    " From this date I shall act accordingly.

" *Date, 29th January.*

" My patrol caught four soldiers belonging to a patrol of Captain Crosley (?) from Fourteen Streams—they were out to catch women and children—viz., three men of the Windsorton Town Guard, and one Regular soldier, and one Cape boy. This boy I have shot ; the whites I have spared—they brought some excuses : ' *Being misled by their officers.*'"

"Caught by my patrol an Englishman, Frank Sudder (?), and two Kaffirs sent out to catch Mrs. Diederiks and Mrs. Schwartz, and families. The two Kaffirs I have shot. The Englishman said he was hired by you at 12s. per day for that purpose. Such low conduct I could never believe from you or any other British officer ; and believe that this Frank Sudder is a low loafer, who did this on his own account.

"I am not bloodthirsty, and also spared his life, although I gave him twenty-five cuts with the stirrup strap, and imprisonment in Petrusburg.

"But now I caution you by sending you this Proclamation. You cannot have any more excuses. I must now do my duty.

"Therefore you can spare innocent blood, and as you also as well as myself must appear before a just God, I shall request you not to proceed with any more horrors.

"European newspapers acknowledge the Proclamation of General de Wet good and just.

"Colonel ——, Hoopstad, writes to his wife :—'I have now an army of seventeen natives, sixteen I have armed,' &c., &c. The same Colonel, and also Captain ——, write *repeatedly* to their wives about our ' native scouts' and 'our armed natives,' so that *every* native shall be shot who comes from your side.

"H. A. ——, Hoopstad, writes in his confidential report ' of envoy of surrender to Boers' ; also, 'I then explained the futility of any hopes based on foreign intervention. My remarks were received with smiles. So also my suggestion that Judge Hertzorg and five other Commandants were flying to German territory. Their whereabouts, I saw, was news to them. The reverse of Clements was, however, mentioned especially by them with *éclat*, and, I expect, exaggeration.'

"Well, now, Colonel Courtenay, you see an infamous lie. Judge Hertzorg is in the Cape Colony and—see the newspapers— he is most successful.

"Is it not terrible ? Broome goes with a special mission to the enemy with such terrible lies, and can you be astonished that one of the Commandants answered him : 'He could not believe any more English Proclamations, as the English do not act accordingly.'

"I shall make known all those lies to all our officers, and tell them never to allow any more meetings of that kind with British civil officers. Bring this to the notice of Lord Kitchener, and tell him that the Hoopstad officers deceive their own nation as well as the enemy, because such frauds will lengthen the war rather than shorten it."

" *Copy.*

"To O.C. Christiana,

" HOOPSTAD, 31*st January*, 1901.

"DEAR SIR,—Myself and others would be grateful to you if you could send a few hundred cigarettes back by the runner ; I would send you cheque by earliest opportunity. Apologising for troubling you over a matter like this.

"Sincerely yours,

"(Sgd.) ——, *Captain,*

"But I sent my runner to Christiana, and he came safely back with 800 cigarettes. It seems that the officers in Hoopstad forget that we have war. They give us splendid opportunities for scouting work.

"To-day I am sending you a certain Rosser ; my patrols caught him near Bloemfontein. I have nothing against him as a spy, therefore I am sending him to you. If I catch him again, then I shall take other measures.

"I have the honour to be,

"Right Honourable Sir,

"(Sgd.) C. C. J. BADENHORST, *Commandant.*
"*District Boshof.*"

" *To all Commanding Officers, Commandants, and Field Cornets of the Burgher Forces.*

"Make known to all burghers, and all whom it may concern, that I, seeing the way this war is carried on in an uncivilised manner by H.M. troops in the O.F.S., by burning of houses, molesting, taking prisoners and carrying off unprotected women and children against their wills, so it is I, Christian Rudolf de Wet, Head Commandant of the O.F.S. Army, do hereby declare that in the future all patrols or persons belonging to the enemy who shall be found to burn houses, or carry off women and children, or if it is shown by good evidence that they intended to do so, I hereby order all commanding officers or burghers to shoot every such person or persons.

> " Given under my hand at the farm Lindeguesfontein (district Kroonstad, O.V.S.), this 2nd day of October, 1900.
>
> > "(Sgd.) C. R. DE WET,
> > " *Head Commandant, O.F.S. Army.*"
>
> > > " *7th February,* 1901.

"— COURTENAY, Esq., *Colonel,*
> " *Commandant, Boshof.*

" SIR,—I beg to state that my boy, now sixteen months uninterruptedly on commando with me, only doing cooking work and looking after my horses, has lately had his house burnt, and wife and children taken away by that gallant '*woman fighter,*' Bruce-Hamilton.

" He was a faithful servant for nearly six years, and only followed me in 1899 to look after me, and had nothing to do with the war. He has changed into a devil now and full of hate to the British nation, and is anxious to avenge his wife and children. He asked me fourteen days' leave of absence to proceed to Cape Colony for the purpose of burning the house of a British subject in accordance. I refused, but I fear he will go one day on his own account. Lots of things of this kind will happen in the future, and who is to blame for all ? Have you ever seen a single house burnt by our people? Kindly make known to the 'inventor of such nonsense proclamations in Johannesburg,' who is directly responsible for such miserable events—Kitchener is fighting the Boers and not the Soudan or savages.

> " I have the honour to be,
> > "Sir,
> > > "Your obedient servant.
> > > > " (Sgd.) F. SCHUYTZE,
> > > > " *Adjutant and Secretary to*
> > > > " *Commandant Badenhorst.*"

Badenhorst's letter evidently contains extracts from his diary, and it will be observed that he refers to letters from Hoopstad which he had captured during the previous week from a despatch rider who was coming to Boshof, but was shot by his captors.

During the remainder of February our scouts were in almost daily contact with the enemy, whose patrols were constantly shelled from the magazine kopjes. Several native families were sent into Boshof by the enemy during the month, being suspected of supplying information to the British.

About this time it became most difficult to obtain wood for fuel, all the timber in the neighbourhood of Boshof having been exhausted, and Merriesfontein Ridge, which was daily occupied by the enemy, being the nearest point where it could be obtained. On the 2nd March a party was sent out to Merriesfontein to cut wood, composed as follows :— All available mounted troops under Lieutenants Johnson and Murphy ; two guns R.F.A., under Lieutenant Mundy ; and eighty of the 4th Scottish Rifles, with Maxim gun, under Captains Clifford and T. K. Gardner, and Lieutenants Thomson-Carmichael, Anderson, and Maxwell-Heron ; the whole, with woodcutters and wagons, under command of Lieut.-Colonel Montague Johnstone. The party occupied Merriesfontein after exchanging shots with the enemy's scouts, who retired, forty of them having been seen. The party returned during the afternoon, bringing with them a large supply of wood, and also a prisoner captured by the Mounted Infantry when scouting near Merriesfontein, Christian Mulke by name. He turned out to be a despatch rider who had lately been with C. de Wet in the Cape

Colony, and he had with him a despatch from Commandant Van-der-Berg to Commandant C. Badenhorst, of which the following is a translation :—

" PETRUSBERG, 28/2/1901.

" The Right Honourable Commandant BADENHORST.

" HONOURABLE SIR,—I have the honour to make known to you that the enemy came to this place with 500 men and three cannon ; I met them with seventy men at Boowel's Plaats. A battle followed, whereby the enemy was defeated with loss of ten dead, three prisoners, fourteen horses killed—three horses, ten saddles, five rifles, and 1000 cartridges taken. Further, that General De Wet is coming back from the Cape Colony.

" Further, you may perhaps have received news already from General Botha.

" With respect, yours,

"(Sgd.) B. VAN DER BERG,
" *Commandant.*"

On the 3rd March a sick convoy proceeded to Kimberley in charge of Civil Surgeon C. A. Loch. Captain J. Campbell Gardner proceeded with this convoy *en route* to Cape Town on sick leave, having been laid up for some time with a severe attack of rheumatism. Civil Surgeon Loch, who had been attached to the battalion since it left Kimberley the previous May, and had made himself most popular with all ranks, proceeded to England on termination of his engagement, and was succeeded by Civil Surgeon A. P. Trinder.

After this the enemy's patrols continued very active as before. One of our scouts was mortally wounded about three miles south of the town on the 8th March, and on the 10th the scouts reported about 300 Boers to the north of the town, which statement was verified by the Staff and Intelligence Officers, but they did not come near enough for any active measures to be taken. Lieutenant Anderson and two scouts were fired on on the same afternoon from Tafel Kop.

On the 18th March a wood-cutting party again went out to Merriesfontein Ridge, composed as before, under Lieut.-Colonel Johnstone, who had with him Lieutenant Johnson, I.Y., and Lieutenant Thomson-Carmichael (the latter having taken over charge of the Mounted Infantry in place of Lieutenant Brudenell Murphy, who had developed enteric fever), Lieutenant Mundy, R.F.A., Captain Mellish, Captain T. C. Gardner, and Lieutenants Forbes, Bridgman, and Anderson. The party came in contact with the enemy's scouts, who retired (one Mounted Infantry horse being killed), and brought 30,000 lbs. of wood. On the 27th March a similar party went out under Lieut.-Colonel Johnstone to Merriesfontein, and, after slight opposition, brought in some 20,000 lbs. of wood.

On Thursday, the 28th March, heavy gun and pom-pom fire was heard to the north at 7 P.M. The Commandant and his staff proceeded out to the twin kopjes, and observed the Kimberley Column in action with the enemy about six miles away. Heliographic communication was established during the afternoon between the magazine kopje and Kameelfontein, where the Kimberley Column was then outspanned, about twelve miles north of Boshof. The O.C. the Kimberley Column heliographed that he would send three wounded men into Boshof the following morning, and asked the Commandant to meet the ambulance and assist it in.   On the following morning (the 29th), in accordance with the message received from the O.C. Kimberley Column, the Commandant and his Staff-Officer, with Lieut.-Colonel Johnstone and Lieutenant Anderson, proceeded at 6 A.M. towards Kameelfontein, taking with them all available mounted men, under Lieutenants Viner Johnson and Thomson-Carmichael.   Having proceeded as far as Rabenthal Farm (nine miles), which they found deserted, and there being no trace of the ambulance, they returned to Boshof, bringing with them some horses, rounded up near Rabenthal.   Heliographic communication with the Column was rendered impossible, owing to clouds and rain.

On the morning of the 30th a helio-message was received from the O.C. Kimberley Column from Kameelfontein, at 6 A.M., stating that the infantry and wagons of the Column were about to start for Boshof, and asking the Commandant to assist them in with his mounted troops. Accordingly the Commandant and his S.O. proceeded out at once with all available Yeomanry and Mounted Infantry to Rabenthal, and occupied all kopjes and ridges between there and Boshof until the infantry and wagons had passed safely in.   The mounted portion of the Kimberley Column arrived in Boshof at about 4 P.M., having made a *détour* to the west, and been engaged with the enemy.   On the following day, the 31st, the mounted troops of the Kimberley Column and guns made a reconnaissance about fifteen miles north, and shelled the enemy from Malaga's Kraal, which had been for some time occupied by a commando.

On the 1st of April the Kimberley Column returned to Kimberley.   The mounted portion of the Column rested at Boshof, while the Commandant and his S.O. took out all his available Mounted Infantry, under Lieutenant Thomson-Carmichael, two guns R.F.A., under Lieutenant Mundy, and 100 of the 4th Scottish Rifles, under Captain Lynch, and escorted the infantry and wagons of the Column as far as Leeuwfontein, where they were subsequently joined by the mounted troops of the Column. Lieutenant Viner Johnson and the men of the Imperial Yeomanry who had been stationed at Boshof for nearly a year, returned to Kimberley with the Column *en route* home and elsewhere; also about fifty time-expired and sick men, the garrison being thus again considerably reduced. The G.O.C. Kimberley District authorised the Commandant to raise an additional number of Mounted Infantry in the battalion, to replace the Yeomanry, and this he proceeded to do forthwith, the Yeomanry having been ordered to leave their horses behind them at Boshof. On this occasion Captain Henning also went to Kimberley with the Column, intending to return to Boshof in a few days, if possible, but this he was unable to do, owing to Boshof being still surrounded by the enemy. Captain T. K. Gardner took over the duties of adjutant during Captain Henning's absence.

Captains Burns-Macdonald and Protheroe Smith, who had returned from England on the expiration of their sick leave, were also detained at Kimberley for the same reason. Captain Macdonald again fell ill, and was subsequently sent down to Cape Town and employed as one of the Staff-Officers for prisoners of war until the embarkation of the battalion for home, while Captain Protheroe Smith was placed in command of the armoured train running between De Aar and Mafeking.

Lieutenant Anderson also proceeded with the Column to

Kimberley on being attached for duty to the Imperial Transport. He had for some months been Garrison Transport Officer at Boshof, and was succeeded in these duties by Lieutenant Maxwell-Heron. On the 2nd April a wood-cutting party, under Lieut.-Colonel Johnstone, composed as before, proceeded to Merriesfontein and returned unopposed with a large supply of wood. While they were still out there a party of the enemy, taking advantage of all mounted men being out of Boshof, appeared on the ridges to the north of the town and began sniping, but were driven off by the D.F.A. guns on the magazine kopje. In the evening a gunner of the 4th Battalion R.F.A. arrived at Boshof and stated that he had been captured from Lord Methuen's Column, near Warrenton, and had been released that morning by 200 of the enemy seven miles north of Boshof.

Skirmishes between our patrols and scouts and those of the enemy continued as usual, and on the 7th of April, 130 of the enemy were reported at Olivierfontein, about six miles south-west of Boshof, their previous movements being unknown. At the same time, one man of the 2nd Battalion Royal Berkshire Regiment arrived at Boshof, having been released by the enemy at Spitzkop, seven miles north-east of Boshof. He stated that he too had been made prisoner from Lord Methuen's Column.

On the 9th April a wood-cutting party, under Lieut.-Colonel Johnstone, again went out to Merriesfontein, composed as follows:—All available Mounted Infantry, under Lieutenant Thomson-Carmichael, two guns 44th Battalion R.F.A., under Lieutenant Mundy, 100 4th Scottish Rifles, under Captain Lynch, Lieutenants Hazlerigg, Forbes, and Maxwell-Heron, with wagons and wood-cutters.

The ridge was occupied without opposition, and three wagon-loads of wood had been cut when one of the scouts galloped in and reported to Lieut.-Colonel Johnstone that a strong force of the enemy was advancing on the ridge from Prisoners' Kopje to the south, and Spitzkop to the north. Lieut.-Colonel Johnstone proceeded to make the necessary dispositions for defence, and sent a despatch to the Commandant, informing him of what had taken place, and the latter proceeded out with his Staff-Officer to Merriesfontein. In the meantime the enemy had opened a heavy fire on the troops from the south and east, to which the Mounted Infantry and Infantry replied, keeping the enemy well in check.   On the arrival of the Commandant, the force had been nearly an hour engaged.   The guns which had been left on the red ridge, about two miles from Merriesfontein, and had been sent for, now galloped up (the infantry escort as far as possible sitting on the limbers), and came into action with time shrapnel at short range, the farm-house of Merriesfontein, into which some of the enemy had been seen to go, being also shelled.   The enemy then retired in more or less confusion, and our force subsequently returned to Boshof, having had only one casualty, thanks to the excellent cover afforded by the large boulders on the ridge, of which the men took every advantage.   The enemy were reported to have had several casualties: one man was seen to be killed, with his horse, by a shell.   At the commencement of the engagement, the wagons which, under Lieutenant Maxwell-Heron, had been sent back to Boshof had a narrow escape of being cut off by a party of the enemy, which had been apparently detached for the purpose, and opened fire on them, but fortunately without effect.   A native who came in on the

16th reported that two of the enemy were wounded, one mortally, in this fight, and that Jacobs's laager had moved from Jaagpan, south of Boshof, to Bank's Drift, on the Modder River.

On the 25th April a wood-cutting party, composed as usual, went out to Merriesfontein and brought in ten wagon-loads of wood. They were unopposed, but saw about 120 of the enemy, whose patrols they shelled. On the 26th April, six despatch riders arrived from Kimberley with a cypher despatch stating that the departure of a convoy from Kimberley with supplies for Boshof had been postponed for ten days. As will be seen later, supplies at this period were becoming very low, and it became necessary to put the inhabitants and garrison on short rations.

On the 27th April, at daybreak, the scouts, when approaching the twin kopjes, were fired upon by the enemy who had occupied the kopjes. During the night one of the scouts was wounded, and two horses killed. The cattle guard of the Mounted Infantry then came out, and the enemy, who on this occasion numbered only 50, retired westward, leaving the farm-house of Kalkfontein, the property of S. Saunders, a refugee in Boshof.

On Tuesday, the 30th April, five men of the 1st East Lancashire Regiment came in and reported that they had been captured by the enemy at Vet River Siding, on the Bloemfontein-Kroonstad Railway, and had been released that morning by the enemy, having been brought down to a laager 7½ miles N.E. of Boshof.

Matters continued as usual, our patrols coming into frequent contact with those of the enemy. On the 6th May a despatch was received from Kimberley that the

F

convoy with supplies for Boshof could not be sent there for a week, and that the inhabitants should be placed on " Starvation Rations," which was accordingly done, the troops also being placed on half a pound of bran bread or biscuit daily. On the same evening a " White Flag " arrived from Jacobs's Commando, with a letter from Commandant Jacobs, begging for some medicines, and such as could be spared were sent out. The bearer of the White Flag was dressed in " Khaki," and Colonel Courtenay wrote to Commandant Jacobs pointing out this fact, and informing him that any of his men found similarly dressed in future would be treated as spies.

On the 10th May, two despatch riders arrived from Kimberley with information from the Intelligence Office that Christian de Wet was moving towards Boshof. The Commandant and S.O. having sighted a Boer patrol from " Loose kopje," about two miles west of Boshof, sent in for two R.F.A. guns, and shelled them off middle kopje, from which they had been watching the cattle guard.

On the 13th May, at 2.45 A.M., despatch riders arrived from Kimberley, with a cypher despatch from the D.A.A.G. to the effect that the Kimberley Column, and convoy for Boshof, had left Windsorton Road on the previous morning, the 12th, and that the G.O.C. wished the Commandant to co-operate with the incoming column, by holding the kopjes north-west of Boshof. Accordingly, at 7 A.M. the Commandant and S.O. proceeded out, and occupied the twin north and loose kopjes, taking with them all the Scottish Rifles Mounted Infantry, under Lieutenant Thomson-Carmichael; two guns R.F.A., under Lieutenant Mundy; and 100 men, Scottish Rifles, under Captain

Clifford, Lieutenants Forbes, Bridgman, and Glossop. On arriving at Loose kopje, the enemy were observed to be holding "Swart Kop" on the Windsorton Road, about six miles from Boshof, and accordingly the Commandant advanced his guns, escorted by the Mounted Infantry, and shelled the enemy off Swart Kop, which he then charged, and took with the Mounted Infantry, holding same and the other ridges until the column and convoy under Major General Pretyman had passed to Boshof. The column had that morning been engaged with the enemy (Erasmus's Commando); four of Dennison's scouts were wounded and five taken prisoners.

On the 14th May, a wood-cutting party again went out to Merriesfontein, under Lieut.-Colonel Johnstone, and brought in a large supply of wood, unopposed, having, however, seen a number of the enemy in the distance.

Major-General T. Pretyman, C.M.G., R.A., the G.O.C. Kimberley district, inspected the station and defences, and expressed himself very pleased with what he saw.

The following day the Kimberley Column with empty convoy left Boshof for Kimberley at 6 A.M.

The G.O.C. inspected the garrison under Colonel A. H. Courtenay at 8.30, and congratulated them "on the excellent work they had done," and upon having "successfully held a corner of the Empire for so long a period."

He also informed the 4th Battalion Scottish Rifles that he was glad to let them know that they would very shortly be relieved and sent home for a well-earned rest.

Colonel Courtenay, who had obtained sick leave, pending embarkation of the battalion for home, then bid farewell to the garrison, and accompanied the G.O.C. to Kimberley, being escorted to join the Column at Leeuwfontein by the Mounted Infantry under Lieutenant Thomson-Carmichael. Lieut.-Colonel Johnstone and Captain A. F. Townsend also accompanied the party to Leeuwfontein. Lieut.-Colonel Johnstone then took over the duties of Commandant from Colonel Courtenay, who had commanded at Boshof, exactly one year, and whose farewell order was as follows :—

"*Station Orders.*

"Boshof, 14*th May,* 1901.

"Colonel A. H. Courtenay feels that he cannot relinquish command of the Boshof Garrison without conveying to all ranks who have served under him for the last twelve months, his sense of the excellent manner in which they have discharged their duties.

"During the last six months these duties have been very arduous, owing to the investment of the town ; but, they have been carried out in a manner which reflects the highest credit on all, and the discomforts which have been consequent on the investment have been cheerfully and uncomplainingly borne.

"The conduct of the N.C.O.'s and men has been exemplary ; and, in bidding farewell to the garrison, Colonel Courtenay begs to thank each one individually for the support he has received, and to wish all God-speed and good luck in the future.

" By Order,

"(Sgd.) A. F. Townsend, *Captain, S.O.*"

It is not given to every one in authority to please all ; and it was with no little satisfaction that the Commandant learned that the services of his battalion and the conduct of all ranks generally had met with the approbation of the civil population. On his relinquishing the command the *Diamond Field Advertiser*, of the 18th May, a Kimberley publication, contained the following pleasing notice :—

"After a residence here of rather more than twelve months the Commandant has left Boshof.

"So far as the town of Boshof is concerned, with its added refugee population, the Commandant has earned grateful thanks for his kindly bearing. Always genial, always hopeful, full of energy, and overflowing with acts of good service to individuals, the memory of his personality will remain, and he may be assured of a hearty welcome should he ever desire to revisit—in friendly times—the scenes of his labour.

"His command, the 4th Battalion Scottish Rifles, have seen a good deal of service in the Orange River Colony. In the neighbourhood of Lindley they passed through some rough experiences, and conducted themselves as good soldiers, and latterly in Boshof they have held the town secure and have had frequent brushes with the enemy."

The men of the D.F.A., under Major May, left Boshof with the Column, handing over their guns to the 4th Scottish Rifles, who supplied crews for them, trained by the R.F.A. Captain Barne, R.E., who had come to Boshof with the Kimberley Column, was left behind with orders from the G.O.C. to construct blockhouses and further defences, with a view to the reduction of the garrison. The introduction of the blockhouse system enabled Lord Kitchener to considerably reduce the garrisons of nearly all the towns. The line of railway was more or less secured, and he had at his disposal a greater number of men to employ with the mobile columns which were scouring the country. The whole of 1901 and part of 1902 were occupied in a series of difficult operations against various Boer leaders, notably Christian de Wet, who eluded with conspicuous skill every effort to capture him. But the "drives" between the long lines of blockhouses eventually wore down the enemy.

Captain Henning, who, as before stated, had been detained at Kimberley on account of the enemy surrounding Boshof, and had been employed on the staff at Kimberley, was appointed acting S.O. to the Kimberley Column, on the 24th April, during the illness of Captain Garton, R.A. Captain Henning continued in this capacity until the departure of the battalion for home.

The Column, when returning to Kimberley with Major-General Pretyman, came in contact with the enemy near Vacht-een-beetje pan, but the latter were soon dispersed by the guns and pom-poms.

A large number of the inhabitants of Boshof left there for Kimberley with this Column. From the 15th until the 21st May the enemy's patrols were as active as usual, and the men of the battalion, not otherwise employed, were occupied in constructing the new defences and block-houses. On the 18th May the scouts were fired on from middle kopje, and a party of the Mounted Infantry, under Lieutenant Thomson-Carmichael subsequently proceeded there with a view to rounding up some loose horses, but were heavily fired upon by an unknown force of the enemy, on the kopje, and obliged to retire.

Early on the morning of the 22nd, scouts arrived from the O.C. Kimberley Column, with a cypher despatch stating that he expected to reach Boshof that morning, and requested the assistance of the Commandant. Accordingly, at 7 A.M., all Mounted Infantry under Lieutenant Thomson-Carmichael, 2 guns R.F.A. under Lieutenant Mundy, and 100 men, 4th Scottish Rifles, under Captain Lynch, and Lieutenants Glossop and Bridgman, proceeded out under Lieut.-Colonel Johnstone, and the S.O., to Leeuwfontein, occupying all the ridges and kopjes in the neighbourhood, which they held till the convoy passed into Boshof at 4 P.M.

The 3rd Battalion Scottish Rifles, under Major Douglas, which had arrived at Kimberley from home, having volunteered to relieve the 4th Battalion, came to Boshof with the Column, and there were cordial meetings between all ranks of the sister battalions. Colonel Farie, commanding the 3rd Battalion, was detained for staff employment at Kimberley.

The Column on its way from Kimberley again met with the enemy near Vacht-een-beetje pan, but dispersed them, it was reported with a loss of eight killed.

The detachment of the 2nd Battalion of the Scottish Rifles, which had been attached to the 4th Battalion since July, 1900, proceeded to Kimberley *en route* to join their own battalion at Greylingstad. They were in charge of 2nd Lieutenant D. C. Sword, who had arrived with the 3rd Battalion from home.

CHAPTER IV.

(17th December 1900 to 24th May 1901.)

SERVICES OF DETACHMENT WITH THE KIMBERLEY FLYING COLUMN.

COLONEL COURTENAY, Commandant at Boshof, having received orders to find 100 men of the battalion for duty with the Kimberley Flying Column, letters C, F, and I Companies were detailed for the purpose, and formed into one company under command of Captain R. W. Mellish and Second Lieutenant A. H. Seagrim.

The detachment left Boshof on the 17th December, 1900, with the Kimberley Column, the latter being under the command of Colonel Parke, Imperial Yoemanry. The other troops composing the column being the Hampshire Yeomanry, Dennison's Scouts, one section 38th Battery R.F.A., one section Pom-poms, one company 2nd Battalion Somersetshire Light Infantry, one company Kimberley Regiment, and one (volunteer) Company Northumberland Fusiliers. On leaving Boshof the Column proceeded to Kimberley, taking with them about ninety Dutch prisoners whom Colonel Courtenay had kept confined in the Dutch Reformed Church for some weeks. The Column arrived at Kimberley without incident on the 19th December, and left again on the 21st for Koffeyfontein, with a convoy *via* Modder River,

72

at which point command was taken over by Colonel Milne, D.S.O., from Colonel Parke ; and passing through Jacobsdal, Koffeyfontein was reached on 26th December, none of the enemy having been encountered *en route.* Leaving Koffeyfontein on the 28th December, the Column, with its detachment of 4th Scottish Rifles, arrived at Modder River on the following evening, and on the 2nd January, 1901, entrained at night for Fourteen Streams, arriving there on the following day, and went into camp, being joined by a detachment of the New Zealand Mounted Infantry. Fourteen Streams was left on 6th January, and Christiana reached on the following day, and on the 8th, the column returned to Fourteen Streams unopposed, and trekked back to Kimberley.

On the 16th January the column started for Boshof with a convoy of about 100 wagons, and on the following day remained at Slabbert's Farm waiting for some steam transport wagons. Small Boer patrols were seen during the day, and were shelled by the pom-poms. On the 18th a start was made for Boshof, and on approaching some kopjes near Wachteen-Beetje they were found to be strongly occupied by the enemy, especially one on the right-hand side of the road, from which the Boers fired heavily on the Yeomanry, killing seven horses ; about a dozen animals in the convoy were also hit. Orders were then given to Captain R. W. Mellish that the Scottish Rifles under his command were to take this kopje. The detachment accordingly advanced against it for some 2000 yards across the open, and, when within about 800 yards, came under a very heavy and well-directed fire. Fortunately the grass was very long, and the men were able to obtain a certain amount of cover from view by lying down half a company at a time, while the other half company "rushed." The company dog which was white and kept moving about in the firing line was hit and had unfortunately to be killed to prevent him from drawing fire on the men.

Eventually, the foot of the kopje being reached, the whole detachment charged with the bayonet; but the enemy declined to wait for them, and the Scottish Rifles, on gaining the summit, could see the Boers galloping off on their horses, some 800 yards away, and were unable to punish them as almost all ammunition was exhausted. Owing to the long grass, the casualties were only three men wounded. Captain Mellish and his men were highly complimented on their work by Colonel Milne, D.S.O., commanding the Kimberley Column, for their pluck and dash under such a heavy fire. Colour-Sergeant Macdonald was obliged to tear the black stripes from his arm, so accurate was the shooting of the enemy.

After a halt at Leeuwfontein the Column trekked again, and arrived at Boshof in the evening, all ridges and kopjes being occupied by the men from Boshof garrison.

On the 20th January, 1901, the Column, with empty convoy, again left Boshof for Kimberley, Captain V. Blake having taken the place of Captain R. W. Mellish, in command of the men of the 4th Battalion Scottish Rifles, and letter "E" Company, taking the place of letter "F" Company.

On the 24th inst., Captain V. Blake being in command of all the infantry in the Column, the latter left Kimberley and proceeded to Koffeyfontein *via* Jacobsdal, a good deal of sniping taking taking place on the way. Leaving Koffeyfontein on the 29th inst., the Column proceeded to Petrusburg, meeting with a little opposition at various points, losing a few men and horses, and arriving back in Kimberley on the 4th February.

On the 9th February the detachment of the 4th Scottish Rifles, with the other infantry of the Column, was sent by train from Kimberley to Orange River, and, being joined there by the mounted troops and guns, proceeded to Zouts Drift, where a position was taken up with a view to cutting off the retreat of Christian de Wet and his force northwards from the Cape Colony.

From this date, until the 3rd March, when it arrived at De Aar, the Kimberley Column was occupied in making marches and counter-marches in the neighbourhood of Orange River Station and Hopetown. · Captain Blake then proceeded in charge of a convoy and 150 men as escort for Prieska, and arrived back at De Aar on the 16th inst., without incident. The Column then returned by train to Kimberley, arriving there on the 19th inst.

On the 20th March Captain V. Blake handed over his command in Kimberley to Captain A. R. C. Littledale. On the 26th March the Column again left Kimberley and proceeded to Kameelfontein, twelve miles north of Boshof; some sharp fighting took place *en route*, five of the Yeomanry being wounded (three mortally). The camp was sniped on the night of arrival at Kameelfontein, and the Column then marched into Boshof, which they left on the 1st April, on the return to Kimberley. The detachment of the Scottish Rifles then accompanied the Column to Koffeyfontein *via* Jacobsdal, and returned *via* Honeynestkloof, having met with a considerable amount of sniping.

The Infantry, under Captain Littledale, then proceeded to Warrenton, and escorted some empty ox-wagons to Kimberley, after which the Column proceeded to Petrusburg, which was then in the hands of the enemy, who, however, evacuated the town on the approach of the troops.   The Column waited at Petrusburg for a few days, there being five Commandoes in the neighbourhood, and then returned to Kimberley *via* Jacobsdal.   A good deal of opposition was met with, it being necessary to shell the enemy off the ridges on frequent occasions, and during some night sniping, Bugler Wilson of the Scottish Rifles was wounded, and one horse of the Scottish Rifles Mounted Infantry was killed.   The Column then proceeded to Windsorton Road, from which place they took a convoy to Boshof on the 13th May, being accompanied by Major-General Pretyman, C.B., commanding the Kimberley District.   On this occasion Dennison's Scouts had nine casualties, and the convoy was assisted into Boshof by the troops from the garrison, under Colonel A. H. Courtenay. The Column then returned to Kimberley, and in three days afterwards left again for Boshof with another convoy and with the 3rd Battalion Scottish Rifles, which relieved the 4th Battalion of the Regiment at Boshof on the 22nd May, the latter Battalion returning with the Column to Kimberley on the 24th May.

While with the Kimberley Flying Column forty men of the detachment of the 4th Scottish Rifles were mounted, and were commanded by 2nd Lieutenant A. H. Seagrim, assisted by Sergeant T. Morris.

On the 27th May the Detachment rejoined the battalion at Alexandersfontein on return to Cape Town for embarkation for home.

CHAPTER V.

(23rd May 1901 to 27th June 1901.)

RETURN TO CAPE TOWN—EMBARKATION FOR ENGLAND—
RECEPTION AT HAMILTON—DISEMBODIMENT—CASUAL-
TIES, HONOURS, AND REWARDS—MEDALS PRESENTED
BY THE KING—CONCLUSION.

AT five P.M., on the 23rd of May, Lieut.-Colonel Johnstone handed over the command at Boshof to Major W. C. Douglas, commanding the 3rd Battalion Scottish Rifles in the absence of Colonel Farie, and the 4th Battalion marched out of the town with the Kimberley Column with orders to make a forced march to Kimberley. Nothing of importance occurred, and the column arrived at Hall's Farm, near Kimberley, on the following evening, after a creditable march of thirty-one miles in twenty-four hours. Thence the battalion proceeded, on the morning of the 26th, to Modder River in charge of an empty convoy, being joined by Captain Henning, who resumed his duties of Adjutant. The battalion was joined at Alexandersfontein by Captain Littledale and the detachment which had been with the Kimberley Column. Captain J. Campbell Gardner and Lieutenant Bridgman were left at Kimberley, the former to rejoin the 3rd Battalion and raise more mounted troops for

Boshof, the latter for duty with the Imperial Transport, to which Lieutenant Anderson had been previously posted. Lieutenant Russell, who had been doing duty for some months with the South African Constabulary, was left with the Kimberley Column, acting in the capacity of Provost-Marshal thereto.

The battalion arrived at Modder River on the 27th May, and received orders to remain there for four or five days; but these orders were countermanded on the following morning, and the battalion entrained for Cape Town at ten A.M. on 28th inst. On the morning of the 30th May they were stopped at Worcester, but left there again the night of the 31st for Cape Town, arriving there the following day and embarking on board H.M. transport *Manhattan* for conveyance to England, Colonel Courtenay reassuming command prior to embarkation. Lieutenant G. Hazlerigg, having unfortunately developed enteric fever just before the departure of the battalion from Boshof, had to be left behind there; and Lieutenant R. Forbes received orders at Cape Town to join the 1st Battalion Highland Light Infantry, to which he had been gazetted.

Lieutenant Thorburn, who had for many months been employed as Assistant Railway Staff Officer at Kimberley, remained there, having been seconded for service on the staff.

The following officers embarked at Cape Town with the battalion, Colonel A. H. Courtenay, commanding:—Major and Hon. Lieut-Col. Montague Johnstone, Major H. Chavasse; Captains, H. M. Clifford, A. R. C. Littledale, D. Blaikie-Hislop, C. J. Lynch, V. A. Blake, D. Burns-Macdonald, H. H. Protheroe Smith, A. F. Townsend,

R. W. Mellish, and T. K. Gardner; Lieutenants, M. H. D. Thomson-Carmichael, R. R. Brudenell Murphy, R. Glossop, B. C. Maxwell-Heron, and A. A. Seagrim; Captain and Adjutant C. M. S. Henning; Lieutenant and Quartermaster W. Taylor; Civil Surgeons, A. P. Trinder and E. L. Mansel. Of the officers of the battalion who went out with it but did not return home with it, and who have not already been accounted for, the following obtained their commissions in the line, and they proceeded to join on being gazetted, viz. :—Lieutenant G. F. Phillips to 2nd Battalion Scottish Rifles, Lieutenant A. F. Lumsden to 2nd Battalion The Royal Scots, Lieutenant H. Boyd-Rochfort to 21st Lancers.

Leaving Cape Town the evening of Saturday, 1st June, the *Manhattan* arrived at Las Palmas at seven P.M. on Wednesday, the 19th, leaving there again that night for Southampton, which was reached on the morning of Wednesday, 26th June. The same evening the battalion entrained for Hamilton, where a very gratifying reception awaited it the following morning; the train arriving amidst a perfect salvo of fog-signals. On the platform, in addition to the friends of the officers and men, were Provost Keith and the Town Council; the former in a well-chosen speech officially welcoming the regiment in the name of the townspeople, and assuring them of the admiration which their good services had attracted at home; finally, he called for three hearty cheers for the battalion. Colonel Courtenay, in thanking the Provost for his kind words of welcome, assured him that the Lanarkshire men had well sustained the high reputation of the Scottish soldier, and that they would always remember the kind reception accorded them by the townspeople of Hamilton. Headed by the band and pipers of the 3rd and 4th Battalions Highland Light Infantry, the battalion made its way through the crowded streets to the barracks, where Colonel Rutherford commanding the 26th and 71st Regimental Districts, welcomed it in the name of Lieut.-General Sir Archibald Hunter, commanding the troops in Scotland, who was officially detained in England. Through the kindness of Provost Keith the men were entertained to breakfast; they afterwards gave in their service uniforms, changed into civilian clothing, and after receiving the balance of their pay, were marched by companies to the station, and like good soldiers returned in a quiet and orderly manner to their homes. It may be added here that on reinforcements being required for the 3rd Battalion, Captain A. R. C. Littledale, eight sergeants, six corporals, and two hundred and three riflemen of the 4th Battalion volunteered to go out a second time to the seat of war, where they saw further active service until the conclusion of peace.

Many of the men of the regiment who so pluckily served their country in South Africa were destined never to return to Scotland. The casualties, a nominal roll of which is given in Appendix B, amounted to fifteen non-commissioned officers and men killed or died of disease, and three officers and six rank and file wounded. This is exclusive of those invalided on account of enteric and other complaints.

In acknowledgment of the services of the battalion in South Africa it received, in common with the rest of the Militia, the thanks of both Houses of Parliament; medals and clasps for the campaign were awarded equally to all ranks; and the battalion had the further honour of being permitted to bear on its appointments the words, "South Africa, 1900–1901."

Six officers and eight non-commissioned officers had the distinction of being mentioned in despatches by Lord Roberts or Lord Kitchener.* Of this number, Colonel Courtenay, commanding the battalion, was created a Companion of the Order of the Bath, Lieut.-Colonel Montague Johnstone received the Distinguished Service Order, while Colour-Sergeant J. Campbell, and Sergeant T. Morris were awarded medals for distinguished conduct on the field. The King was further pleased to honour the battalion by commanding the attendance of the Officers and Permanent Staff at Marlborough House to receive their war medals from His Majesty in person. In the presence of Her Majesty the Queen and the members of the Court, this gratifying ceremony took place at 3 P.M., on the 29th July, 1901. The names of the officers and men present are given in Appendix D.

The foregoing pages will show that the 4th Battalion of the Scottish Rifles experienced a fair share of the trials and hardships of the South African campaign, and worthily maintained the credit of the distinguished regiment of which it has the honour to form a part.

The conduct of all ranks in quarters, on the march, and under fire, won the openly expressed approval of Lieut.-General Lord Methuen, Major-General Pretyman, C.M.G., Major-General Paget, and all under whom the battalion served; while their endurance of every kind of hardship and discomfort was worthy of the highest praise. The detachment which served with the 20th Brigade during its three months' operations in the Orange Free State, from May to

---

* See Appendix C.

August, 1900, were often on the shortest rations for days at
a time, while the men suffered severely from exposure to the
cold at night; many of them had nothing but Khaki drill
clothes, their shirts and underclothing being nearly worn
out. At times the frost was so severe that it was impossible
to get breakfast until the sun had risen sufficiently to melt
the ice in the water-barrels, fuel being next to impossible to
obtain. During the six months' investment of Boshof, officers
and men slept the whole time in the trenches, which during
the wet season were often flooded, thunderstorms, with heavy
rain, being at the time of almost daily occurrence, and the men
on outpost duty being often wet through in consequence.

The vigilance and steadiness of the N.C.O.'s and men
during this trying period, and the manner in which they
worked at the defences of Boshof, which had to be frequently
altered owing to reductions in the garrison, was beyond all
praise; while to the excellent manner in which the trenches
were made, is mainly due the small number of casualties
which occurred in the battalion.

In common with the inhabitants of Boshof, officers and
men alike experienced, during the latter part of their stay
there, many of the privations of a siege. Such necessaries
as soap, matches, butter, sugar, &c., were unobtainable, while
liquor of any description was unheard of, from January to
May, except in hospital.

Before the arrival of the convoy in May, the men's
clothing and boots were worn out, many of them being
obliged to wear civilian clothing commandeered in the
town. The greatest privation of all, however, was being cut
off for so long from the outer world; only occasionally was it
possible to get despatch riders to and from Kimberley. It

was a matter of great danger and difficulty throughout the whole investment, and especially for the first six weeks or two months, when it was practically impossible, and no letters or newspapers were received from home or elsewhere. War and newspaper correspondents were unheard of at Boshof after the 1st Division left in May, 1900, and, consequently, Boshof was as little heard of by the outer world as the latter was by the inhabitants of Boshof.

So long as the district remained peaceful, the officers, with the true British sporting interest, did their best to brighten their men and the lives of the inhabitants. From June till September, 1900, the officers enjoyed capital sport of every description, for springbok, steinbok, partridge, karan, hares, &c. were plentiful; several officers were also able to obtain good specimens of the wildebeest and hartebeest. Many of the Burghers in the district were most hospitable in inviting the officers to stay with them, and did their best to afford good sport.

Polo was improvised, for which the officers had to break their own ponies. In a match at Kimberley against the 5th Battalion Royal Dublin Fusiliers, in August, 1900, Captain Henning and Lieutenants Thomson-Carmichael, Lumsden, and Bridgman, representing the 4th Battalion Scottish Rifles, had the satisfaction of winning by five goals to two.

The N.C.O.'s and men, during the whole period of their stay at Boshof, spent most of their spare time at cricket; but football, the national game of Scotland, was the popular recreation. No matter how tired the men were, they managed to retain enough energy to kick the ball about. The Inter-Company matches were keenly contested, and there is no doubt the game did much to brighten the otherwise dull lives of the men.

A gymkhana was organised in the autumn, which culminated in a small race meeting later on, for which the prizes were provided by the officers. It attracted some excellent racing ponies from Kimberley and elsewhere. Captain Fergusson, Provost-Marshal at Kimberley, was one of the most successful winners, while Mr. De Vet, of Hartebeest Pan, Boshof District, with his pony "Early," won the Burgher's Silver Cup (presented by the officers for horses the property of Burghers in the district).

The Sports were generally followed in the evening by a Concert in the Town Hall, in which the ladies and gentlemen resident in Boshof, Dutch as well as English, took part with the officers and men of the garrison. These gatherings were most successful, and were much appreciated, but were brought to an abrupt conclusion on the arrival of news of the cowardly way in which the inhabitants of Jacobsdal behaved towards the troops, when that place was attacked by the enemy in October. No amusements of this description were possible during the investment, but the officers made a lawn tennis and croquet ground in the centre of the town, of which the inhabitants were invited to make use, and gladly availed themselves. Shortly before the departure of the battalion from Boshof, the state of affairs being less critical, the officers organised a farewell Gymkhana, particulars of which may not be uninteresting to some readers, and are therefore given in Appendix B.

This account of the Battalion's work would be incomplete without some reference to the services of the Medical Staff at Boshof, under Major Peard, R.A.M.C., who had charge of the Hospital when the 1st Division left Boshof. Nothing was left undone to alleviate the suffering and promote the comfort of the patients who at that time numbered over 200 sick and wounded, in a hospital at first very badly equipped. Major Peard was ably assisted by Civil Surgeons Lock and Peare, and subsequently by Civil Surgeon Suffield. And when Major Peard left Boshof for Bloemfontein in August, 1900, he was relieved by Lieutenant Dinnis, R.A.M.C., who carried out the duties ably and efficiently, assisted by Dr. Lock until the latter's return home, when Dr. Trinder succeeded him. Dr. Brownlow (who was a refugee at Boshof for some time with Mrs. Brownlow and their family) was also most kind, giving his valuable services and experience in consultation with the other medical men in several serious cases of wounds and illness. The devotion of Nursing Sisters, the Honourable Florence Colborne, Good, and Palmer, will not easily be forgotten by those who were under their care. Their invariable kindness and cheerfulness during many a weary and trying hour did much to alleviate the sufferings and raise the spirits of the sick and wounded.

Mention must also be made of Captain R. H. Robinson, Army Service Corps, who was in charge of supplies, &c. from the 30th July, 1900, and was indefatigable in the discharge of his important duties, which were by no means light, especially during the investment, when he had to provide food for the inhabitants as well as the troops. He was a welcome and esteemed Honorary Member of the Mess of the Scottish Rifles.

The South African War is the ninth occasion within the last century and a half that the Militia force has been embodied for permanent duty on account of some national emergency. Though the fact is soon forgotten, on each of these occasions the services of the force have been of a nature entitling it to the gratitude of the nation. It is the oldest military body in the kingdom, and has never failed the country. The public has not sufficiently realised that the Militia was in no sense bound to serve out of England. The non-commissioned officers and men, the majority of them in poor circumstances, of their own free will broke up their homes, and gave up their work in many cases to their subsequent ruin, to risk their lives for their country. The Militia of North Britain showed up well during the war. It is hoped that Scotsmen will not forget this, and in particular that Lanarkshire people will not forget the service of their county regiment.

APPENDICES.

---•---

APPENDIX A.

General de Villebois Mareuil's Orders for Attack on Boshof, 4.4.00.

Cette nuit le détachement de raid attaquera Boshof et poursuivra ensuite sa route à la faveur de la surprise et de l'obscurité. A cet effet les dispositions suivantes seront observées. La colonne partira à 4 h. de l'après-midi avec le détachement des Boers du Field Cornet Daniells de la manière à pénétrer seulement á la nuit sous les vues de Boshof. A un point de la route les deux détachements bifurqueront et gagneront leur place de rassemblement respective à l'est et à l'ouest de la ville. Celle-ci se présente dans une plaine et se trouve flanquée de quelques kopjies, dont l'importance et la proximité sont aussi rapportées. Au nord deux kopjies vues et à peine gardées à une assez bonne distance de la ville et entre lesquelles passe la route Hoopstadt-Boshof. Elles seront tournées sans qu'on les occupe. A l'ouest sur la route de Kimberley qu'elle commande, une kopjie qui n'est pas gardée par l'ennemi et sur laquelle les Boers prendront position. Enfin au sud-est de la ville et tout contre une kopjie, où les Anglais ont un poste d'une cinquantaine d'hommes, et dont ils ont couronné le sommet d'un petit parapet de pierres à une hauteur d'homme, elle fera partie du plan d'attaque réservé au détachement de raid.

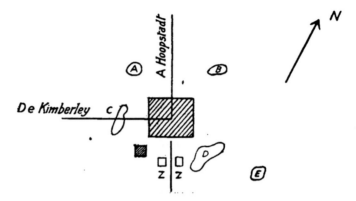

Les deux routes de Hoopstadt et de Kimberley se croisent dans l'intérieur de la ville. Le plan d'attaque sera exécuté dans les conditions ci-après.

A 11 heures soir les Boers du Field Cornet Daniells seront en position sur la kopjie C. et le fil télégraphique qui suit la route de Kimberley aura été coupé par eux.

A la même heure le détachement de raid sera rassemblé derrière la kopjie E., située à 2 kilomètres de la ville. Les chevaux et la Scotch-cart y attendront le fin de l'opération. Il sera laissé, en y comprenant les boys personnels s'il en existe, un homme par groupe de six chevaux. On désignera avant départ ces hommes, dont la mission de confiance n'échappera à personne puisque de leur vigilance dépendrait le salut de l'expédition en cas de retraite. La groupe laissée à la place de rassemblement sera sous les ordres de *Nicollet.* Les hommes resteront debout à la tête des chevaux sellés et bridés, les boys du cart à la tête des mules attachées.

A 11 heures et ¼ le détachement d'attaque se mettra en marche en 3 échelons à 20 mètres de distance, le centre en avant. L'échelon du centre sous ma direction plus spéciale sera formé du peloton français. L'échelon de droit comprendra la moitié des Hollanders, l'échelon de gauche l'autre moitié. En outre les Cavaliers du Raid qui ont formés des groupes pour la mise en

commun des vivres et de la cuisine se désigneront un chef de
groupe dont à aucun prix il ne se séparerait.

Au cas où ces groupements n'existraient pas on dépasseraient
10 hommes, les chefs de détachements opéreraient un frac-
tionnement par 6 ou 8 hommes avec désignation de chef de
groupe.

Dans la marche d'approche, les commandements se feront à mi-
voix, les hommes en ligne sur un rang pour voir le chef et se con-
centrer instantainement. Il importe en effet d'observer les in-
vestigations de l'héliographe au cas où les Anglais en posséderaient
un à Boshof, ce qui n'est pas encore prouvé. Au moment où le
rayon va se tourner sur l'échelon le chef fait coucher son monde et
la marche n'est reprise qu'hors de la reconnaissance lumineuse. A
hauteur de la kopjie D. ou s'arrêtera derrière le cimetière, l'échelon
de droite se portera alors à l'assant de la kopjie et l'occupera. De
là il tiendra sous son feu les deux kraals Z. Z., où les Anglais
campés sur la place du marché, dans Boshof même, pouvraient se
jeter d'abord pour tenter de résister. En aucun cas, pour un
motif facile à comprendre, il ne sera tiré sur la ville. Le feu
d'ailleur ne sauraient être admis que de tout près dans les conditions du commandement si précises qu'il ne soit exécuté que des
feux de salve.

Les deux autres échelons poursuivraient leur marche, passeront
derrière les kraals, et attaqueront le camp anglais, situé hors de la
ville. A cet effet l'échelon français après deux feux de salve, se
précipitera au pas de charge au cri " *Transvaal Free State,*" et
complétera la panique. Après avoir traversé le camp, on prendra
position sur la face sud, et on achevera la déroute par des feux.
Les Boers placés sur la route de Kimberley sur la kopjie C.
recevront les fuyards. Il est probable que le camp anglais placé
dans Boshof se retirera simplement sur Kimberley, mais il
pourrait arriver 'qu'il essayat de recouvrir le camp attaqué en
sortant de Boshof par la route de Kimberley pour tourner
l'attaque.

Elle serait alors informée de cette éventualité par le détachement du Field Cornet Coleman qui couvrira la gauche de
l'attaque.

Pour se reconnaître on couvrira la calotte du chapeau avec un mouchoir blanc.

La force anglaise à Boshof varie entre 300 et 400 hommes.

Quoiqu'il arrive, les assaillants doivent se rappeler que leur supériorité morale est écrasante et que même, en cas de retraite, ils ont toute facilité, la nuit, pour rattrapper leurs chevaux, et s'éloigner sans risques de Boshof.

APPENDIX B.

Nominal Roll of Casualties in the 4th Battalion Scottish Rifles during its service in South Africa, 1900–1901, not including those in the detachment of the 2nd Battalion, which was attached to the 4th Battalion from July 1900 to May 1901.

DIED OR KILLED IN ACTION.

OFFICERS, *nil.*

N.C.O.'s AND MEN.

No.	2757	Sergeant	Philip Egan.
	2112	Corporal	John M'Cartney.
	153	„	Thomas Mulrooney.
	215	Private	John Allan.
	1943	„	Archibald Ballock.
	8066	„	Donald Douglas.
	6013	„	Angus Ferguson.
	2433	„	Joseph Grieve.
	6545	„	John Harvey.
	2443	„	John M'Allister.
	8640	„	James M'Palland.
	432	„	David May.
	5026	„	John Murphy.
	600	„	William Murphy.
	1755	„	Alexander Wilkie.

WOUNDED.

OFFICERS.

Captain D. Blaikie-Hislop.
Lieutenant R. R. W. Brudenell Murphy.
Second Lieutenant H. Boyd-Rochfort.

N.C.O.'s AND MEN.

No. 9632 Lance-Corpl. Patrick Davidson.
„ 5701 Bugler Maurice Wilson.
„ 2835 Private Alexander Gardner.
„ 5013 „ James Irvine.
„ 2554 „ William Monaghan.
„ 5830 „ James Robertson.

APPENDIX C.

NAMES OF OFFICERS AND NON-COMMISSIONED OFFICERS MENTIONED IN DESPATCHES.

Colonel A. H. Courtenay,
Hon. Lieut.-Colonel M. G. Johnstone,
Captain and Adjutant C. M. S. Henning,
Captain A. F. Townsend,
Lieutenant R. R. W. B. Murphy, •
2nd Lieutenant H. Boyd-Rochfort, } By Field-Marshal LORD ROBERTS.
Colour-Sergeant J. Campbell,
Sergeant T. Morris,
„ T. M'Leod,
„ J. Wilson,
Corporal J. Dailly,
„ J. Higgins,

Captain A. F. Townsend,
Lieutenant R. R. W. B. Murphy, } By General LORD KITCHENER.
Colour-Sergeant T. E. Rowe,
„ A. E. Slade,

APPENDIX D.

Names of Officers, N.C.O.'s, and Men of Permanent Staff who received War Medals at Marlborough House from His Majesty The King.—3 p.m., 29th *July*, 1901.

Colonel A. H. Courtenay.
Hon. Lieut.-Colonel M. G. Johnstone.
Major H. Chavasse.
Captain H. M. Clifford.
    ,,   D. Blaikie-Hislop.
    ,,   C. J. Lynch.
    ,,   A. F. Townsend.
    ,,   A. R. C. Littledale.
    ,,   Burns-Macdonald.
    ,,   R. W. Mellish.
    ,,   V. A. Blake.
Lieutenant R. R. W. B. Murphy.
    ,,   M. H. D. Thomson-Carmichael.
    ,,   G. Hazlerigg.
Captain and Adjutant C. M. S. Henning.
Lieutenant and Quartermaster W. Taylor.
Sergeant-Major C. Buchanan.
Quartermaster-Sergeant C. W. Clarke.
Orderly-Room-Sergeant H. C. Saich.
Colour-Sergeant T. Irvine.
    ,,   C. Nairn.
    ,,   D. M'Donald.
    ,,   T. Wilson.
    ,,   E. Rowe.
    ,,   H. Cummings.
    ,,   A. E. Slade.
    ,,   J. Campbell.
    ,,   H. Duncombe.
Lance-Corporal J. Gordon.
Sergeant-Bugler Sullivan.

Bugler H. Wood.
   „   Chaffey.
Sergeant T. Degnan.
   „   T. M'Leod.
   „   T. Norris.

.The remainder of the Officers and Permanent Staff were unavoidably absent on furlough and unwell.

APPENDIX E.

From the DIAMOND FIELDS ADVERTISER, KIMBERLEY, *Saturday, May* 18, 1901.

BOSHOF NOTES.

GARRISON SPORTS.

By kind permission of the Commandant, garrison sports were held on 9th May, when the following judges, starters, and clerks discharged their duties with justice, precision, and courtesy :—

Judges : Lieut.-Colonel Montague Johnstone, 4th Scottish Rifles ; Captain Ross, District Commissioner. Starters : Captain Gardner, 4th Scottish Rifles ; Lieutenant Mooy, Town Guard. Clerks of the Course : Captain Robinson, O.C., Army Service Corps ; Captain Clifford, 4th Scottish Rifles. Hon. Treasurer and Secretary : Lieutenant Dinnis, Royal Army Medical Corps.

The programme and results were as follows :—

Flat Race for Officers.—Ponies, 14·1. Three furlongs. Catch weights—Lieutenant Bridgman's Tommy, 1 ; Lieutenant Dinnis' ——, 2 ; Captain Lynch's Fattie, 3.

Garrison 100 *Yards Race.*—1, Sergeant M'Geary, 4th S.R. ; 2, Private Rothman, D.F.A. ; 3, Private M'Williams, A.S.C.

Scottish Rifles 100 *Yards Race.*—1, Private Haig, " Details " 2nd S.R. ; 2, Private J. Hamilton, 4th S.R. ; 3, Sergeant M'Geary, 4th S.R.

On 11th May a race, the outcome of this, was run between Sergeant M'Geary and Private J. Hamilton for stakes of £5.

Won by the Sergeant, after a brilliant run, the second being little more than one foot behind.

Officers Flat Race (100 yards). 1 yard for each year's service.— 1, The Commandant, Colonel Courtenay, 30 yards ; 2, Lieut.- Colonel Montague Johnstone, 28 yards ; 3, Captain Ross, D.C., 15 yards. This race excited great interest and much friendly comment. The Commandant won in grand style ; Colonel Johnstone covered the ground with giant stride, and Captain Ross finished with any amount of reserve "wind." In addition to the winners the following entries were made : — Captain Robinson, O.C., A.S.C. ; Major Chavasse, S.R. ; Captain Lynch, S.R. ; Captain Gardner, S.R. ; Lieutenant Dinnis, R.A.M.C.

N.C.O.'s and Men's Sack Race (60 yards).—1, Private Black, 4th S.R. ; 2, Private Gould, "Details" 2nd S.R. ; 3, Private J. Sutherland, 4th S.R. A capital race ; winner finished with a good lead.

Tug-of-War.—In heats. Teams of eight. 4th S.R. team beat A.S.C. team. S.R. winning team were : Sergeant R. M'Geary (captain), Lance-Corporal Paterson, Lance-Corporal Currie, Private Dickson, Private Paterson, Private Hughes, Piper Green, Private Kirsick, Private Mitchell.

Hurdle Race for Officers' Ponies. — 14·1 and under. One mile, Catch weights. Colonel Courtenay's O'Brien (Lieutenant Carmichael), 1 ; Lieutenant Carmichael's Polly (Lieutenant Mundy, R.A.), 2. Lieutenant Bridgman's Tommy finished first, but was disqualified for running out. A well-contested race, but the hurdles were thin, owing to the scarcity of bushes, and rather encouraged the ponies to leave the course. The Colonel's pony started favourite. It was well ridden, and steadily accomplished all that was expected.

Veterans' Race.—For N.C.O.'s, fourteen years' service, one yard for every year over : 1, Sergeant M'Geary, S.R. ; 2, Sergeant Duncombe, S.R.

Three-legged Race (150 yards).—1, Gunner Payne and Gunner Houth, 44th Batt., R.F.A. ; 2, Private M'Phee and Private Gould, 2nd S.R. ; 3, Driver Prince and Driver Rothman, D.F.A. A really good race ; winners came in well without a false step.

Thread the Needle Race.—1, The Commandant and Mrs. Hammelberg ; 2, Lieutenant Mundy, R.A., and Mrs. Louis Beck ; 3, Lieutenant Carmichael and Miss Jacobs. Colonel Courtenay, by winning this race, scored his third event in the day's sport.

Donkey Sweepstake.—Costume optional. 1, Private T. O'Niell, M.I., S.R. ; 2, Gunner Payne, R.A. A large entry ; a motley assembly of donkeys ; some would go, some would not ; some ran to the right, some to the left ; some went towards the goal along the course or through the excited crowd, and not a few went in the opposite direction.

On May 11 a "Place Kicking" competition took place, with the following result :—1, Private Willis, 54 yds. 1 ft. 9 in. ; 2, Corporal Hartley, 48 yds. 1 ft. 10 in. ; 3, Private Gould, 47 yds. 1 ft. 8 in.

LORIMER AND CHALMERS, PRINTERS, EDINBURGH.

CPSIA information can be obtained at www.ICGtesting.com
Printed in the USA
LVOW08s1956090215

426300LV00038B/3039/P